A Million Miles

with

Big

Bad

GOOD

Bob

A Million Miles with Big Bad GOOD Bob

Big Bob as told to Jody Dyer

Crippled Beagle Publishing
Knoxville, Tennessee
dyer.cbpublishing@gmail.com

Cover design by Marcy Gooberman, www.marcygooberman.com

Paperback ISBN 978-1-970037-29-6
Hardcover ISBN 978-1-970037-30-2
eBook ISBN 978-1-970037-33-3

Library of Congress Control Number: 2019920462

In a contemporary memoir, stories are told as the author can best recall. Dialogue, events, and dates in this life story are as accurate as possible given the frailties of the human memory. Some names have been changed to protect individuals' privacy. Regardless, the soul is the soul, and the author prays that readers understand his message and find hope and a future no matter your backgrounds, choices, health conditions, or personal circumstances.

Printed in the United States of America

If you've never been on a chopper, you really don't know what you're missing. There's nothing better than going down the road well in excess of 100 miles an hour. Just running down the road. I never had a speedometer. I got chased. About half the time, I got away. Yes, crazy, crazy days.

—Big Bob, Dartmouth-Hitchcock Medical Center
New Hampshire, March 2019

DYING

THEY DOUBLED UP MY DILAUDID. It wasn't killing the pain. I can take a half-tablet without getting too sick, but I've had a headache now for three days, so they told me to take the whole pill. Now I'm having to get used to eight milligrams. It's like heroin. The first stuff was bad, but this is worse. Actually, I take a whole cup of different pills, and some get stuck down at the base of my throat. When I have to take them, I make sure my stomach is full of food. If I don't hold my head in a certain position, the medicine makes me throw up. It's all strong stuff. Every time I get home from the doctors, I have to lie down. I'm tired.

I've been getting up at five in the morning to go to dialysis on Monday, Wednesday, and Friday from six to eleven. I went a few days without dialysis, and they took out five kilograms of fluid the next time I went. All the stuff you eat is supposed to be filtering out of your body through your kidneys, but when you don't have that, and you wait too long to do dialysis, it builds up and has a really bad effect on you. At the dialysis center, the water in your body goes out and through a machine and then gets cleaned and put back in. I just sit in that chair for five hours. It's really hard, the leather recliner, and it kills my lower back. After the first hour of treatment, my back starts throbbing. Sometimes, I have to sit down and stand up over and over so they can get my blood pressure right. Sometimes, I have to take in more fluid because my blood pressure gets so low. I still don't feel good after that. I can't sleep; I'm in too much pain to sleep. I'm tired.

My doctor says I'm close to the end of treatment. He apologized for starting the dialysis so late. He said if I can stick it out for two more months of dialysis, I might feel better, but right now I just feel like I'm at the end of my line. Two more months is a long time when you feel like I do.

I talked to him about stopping dialysis. He warned me that I'd live only about two weeks after that. I can't go on like this, though. I can't take a shower because of the port in my chest. My doctor bandages the port up better than they do at the dialysis center. He puts a plastic thing over it so I can get a shower. At the dialysis center they just put tape on. I guess I could shower, but it's risky because one port line goes directly into my heart. If it gets wet, it can leak bacteria into the tube. I don't like being dirty, but if that happens, the bacteria will go all through my body and the doctors won't be able to do anything to help me. I don't have a place to shower, anyway. I live in my motor home in the church parking lot. If I had a shower in my motor home, I could at least stick my head in and wash my hair and my beard and my legs.

I have to move. My old motor home will be murder in the winter because the furnace doesn't work. I'm not sure where I'll go just yet when I get out of the hospital. I met with case workers and signed a whole bunch of papers. One is from here at Dartmouth-Hitchcock. They are all trying to get me in an assisted living center that is close to dialysis. I was hoping to get approved for housing, but now they tell me it's a twelve to 48-month waiting period. I meet my case workers every Monday. There's a big demand for housing, but I am on a priority list. Hopefully, they can do something. The church is giving me an extension and letting me stay in my camper in the parking lot until I'm settled in the assisted living. It's September as I write this, and it's cold here in the winter. There just has to be a vacancy. I applied in Canaan, Enfield, and White River Junction, as well as here in Lebanon. I'm getting Meals On Wheels and stuff like that, but the main problem is housing.

Once I move, I'll give my motor home away. I know a young lady who's been looking for one. I'll give it to her. It's old, an '89, but it's got only 35,000 miles on it. It's got a couple minor things to fix up, and I'll start those repairs next week when I'm up to it. I have to get it back in alignment, too. An air suspension problem caused one of the lines to come off. That's nothing. I'll fix it. She can drive it anywhere.

I got more bad news from the doctors. They found that four inches of my aorta are blocked off tighter than a drum. That's why I'm getting no blood to my legs. That's why it hurts to walk. They don't know what they will be able to do about that. I have to do a stress test, and I may need bypass surgery, but the doctors have to make sure my heart's strong enough to go through the test and the surgery. First, they plan to do some kind of strange stress test using chemicals. I really just want this port thing out of my chest so I can shower.

I'm hurting. I'm tired. I look at my life ahead, and all I see is darkness. I don't see light. I'm doubling up on my anti-depressants. If that doesn't help and I don't feel better after two months of dialysis, I'm stopping it. I can't go on like this. The doctors can make me comfortable until the end.

If I just had a little piece of land where I could put this motor home, somewhere with electricity and water and heat, I'd be happy. If I had boatloads of money, I wouldn't be in this predicament. It gives you self-assurance when you don't have to depend on anybody else, when you can take care of yourself. If the social workers don't find me someplace to go, I guess Black Cat and I will be living in the truck again.

I got Black Cat's paperwork all done today so now he's a service cat. That'll be good for me. My doctor fixed it up. I can take Black Cat anywhere I go. I got a leash, but he doesn't like walking. He'd rather have me pick him up and put him over my shoulder.

He's three years old. He's such a good cat. He's very loving. I got him when he was a kitten. Actually, he chose me.

I was sitting in my motor home one day having coffee, and I just happened to look up. I have a curtain across the front windshield, and I saw a mouse climbing up the cloth. I don't like mice. A few days later, I was talking to my niece. I mentioned, "Jess, do you know anybody who's got some kittens they want to get rid of?"

She said, "Why? Do you want a kitten?"

I said, "Yes, I've got to get one. I've got mice in my camper, and I don't like mice."

She said, "Well, it just happens I took in a stray. The mom is just this little bitty thing, but she had three kittens. One is black and two are tigers. I'll bring them down to you."

She brought them down a while later. She set them on the floor about ten feet away from me. Black Cat took a look at me and right away ran and got on my shoes. He climbed up my leg and started purring, so I picked him up and he purred and rubbed his tiny head through my beard.

Jess said, "Which one do you want?"

I said, "I got no choice. He chose me." You always go with the animal that chooses you. I had to wait for two more weeks and then I brought him home for good. He's a one-person cat and doesn't like other animals. He growls at them. He's a good mouser and is totally housebroken. He is so housebroken and trained that when I take him outside, he holds it. If he's got to go to the bathroom, he holds it until he comes back in and goes in the litter box. He likes riding in the truck. The only thing is, if he stands up and he's looking out the window sideways and everything's going by him, he'll get sick. A week ago, he was riding in my truck. He saw a cat about a hundred feet away. He jumped up on the dash and growled and growled. He's loyal.

Black Cat saved my life. I'm Type II diabetic and insulin-dependent. When I came back to Massachusetts 22 years ago, my A1C was out of control. I knew I was sick, but we couldn't get it right. It's supposed to be between six and seven, and at times it was up to twelve and over 10. They say over 10 is coma level and I was always over 10. Just a few weeks after Black Cat moved in with me, I went to the doctor and, for the first time since I was diagnosed with diabetes, my A1C was 6.4.

Black Cat lost about a third of his weight the last time I was in the hospital. He was 30 pounds before I left, and he's down to twenty now. He always waits for me at the door, but when I came back from the hospital, I walked in, and he was on the bed. I figured he thought it was just somebody coming to feed him. When I yelled, "Where's my Black Cat?" he JUMPED off the bed and came running across the floor. I leaned over and he put his paws up on my chest. He purred and rubbed his head all over me. He was really glad to see me.

The folks in the church said that while I was in the hospital Black Cat howled and howled. They heard him day and night. He must have strained his voice because he can hardly meow now, and he used to be really loud. Without Black Cat, I'm here by myself. I have nobody else. I need to find a good home for my cat when I move to assisted living. I'm really gonna miss my kitty.

I can't believe how low I feel . . . being ready to give up, but as I say that aloud or write it down, I get mad. That's what it takes to survive sometimes—getting mad.

My back is against the wall, but when I'm in a fight and my back is against the wall, I usually wind up winning because I don't quit. I fight. It's not in me to quit. I'm not that way. My whole life has been one crazy stunt.

TOUGH

I STARTED FIGHTING WHEN I WAS SIX YEARS OLD. I was in first grade. It happens that my dad's name starts with three letters from a curse word, which got me a lot of harassment. Plus, my mom was always moving us around the area of Worcester, Massachusetts. She'd find tenement houses that were trashed. She'd make a deal with the landlord. He'd buy the materials, and we would fix up the apartment. We cleaned, painted, and made repairs. He'd give us free rent for so many months, maybe four or five. I was a little kid and was hanging wallpaper and scraping and painting ceilings. When we had to start paying rent, Mom could afford a month or two. In those two months she'd find the next apartment or house to rent. Worcester is a big area, so every time we moved, we changed schools.

We lived on Southford Street when I was in first grade. I was walking home from school one day and this gang of kids jumped me. There were seven of them. A couple were sixth graders. I don't think any of them were my age. They were all older, and they whooped the shit out of me.

I went home crying to my mom. As she was cleaning me up, she said, "How many were there?"

I said, "Well, about seven, and they were all older than me."

She said, "How many did you put down?"

I asked, "What do you mean?"

She said, "How many did you knock out?"

I was like, "I didn't knock any out, there were too many of them. They were big."

She got mad and asked me, "You didn't fight for yourself? You didn't stand up for yourself?"

I said, "There were too many."

Oh boy, she dropped my drawers and paddled my bottom and then sent me out and said, "You go find them now, and you fight every one of them. Don't come back till you've fought them all. Whether you win or lose, you fight every single one. You stand up for yourself."

I figured I'd rather get my butt whooped by a gang of guys than her. My mom used to build rubber rafts during the war. She had an arm on her that would make Arnold Schwarzenegger jealous. At work, she was always pulling that rubber and holding it. She had muscles on her. She used to wrestle with me, and it wasn't until I was thirteen or fourteen years old that I finally was able to pin her down.

So, I went out in the neighborhood and tracked those kids down. I actually whooped two of them. Pretty soon after that they came to see me and asked me to be a part of their gang.

I learned really quickly, by about the second grade, to be a good fighter. Find the toughest guy there, get in a fight with him, and put him down.

When I went through grade school, people were always making fun of my last name. You know how vicious kids can be. The best way to end that, especially at a new school, is to wait until recess and then find the toughest guy of all. The toughest guy of all would always be the biggest bully, but also the biggest coward. Bullies don't want to take a chance at being whooped, so they talk big. As soon as one started mouthing off to me, I'd jack him. Hit him. Knock him out. That would usually work, and everybody else would just back off and say, "We don't want part of this guy. He's too crazy." That generally worked, but sometimes it didn't, and I'd have to get into a brawl. It suited me just fine. I didn't go looking for trouble, but I didn't run from it either.

We would have rumbles in the parks. Ever seen *West Side Story*? That's exactly what it was like. We were lower class and poor, but we were tough. I remember going to bed hungry at night. I remember at Christmas time we couldn't even afford a tree, much less presents. I remember standing in front of someone else's tree one year and making a promise. I promised God that when I got older, if I knew of families who were hungry, I'd do whatever I had to do to feed them, and if I knew of kids who weren't going to have any Christmas presents, I'd make sure they had Christmas presents.

BROKEN

I WAS BORN JULY 31, 1947. I am the oldest of Margaret's four children. My sister Joni is next. Her birthday is in February. There was one time in the year where she would catch up at her birthday and we'd be the same age until my birthday, and then I would jump ahead of her another year. Then came my brother Paul and after him, Donnie.

In 1954 doctors diagnosed my brother Paul with Hodgkin's disease. He was four years old. They gave him five years to live. They didn't have any treatment for Hodgkin's disease back in those days. For Paul, they hit him with X-ray treatments. They hit him with so many that he looked like an African-American. His skin turned really dark.

Right after Paul was diagnosed, my dad left. I don't have any memories of my dad except the day my parents split up, which was right after Paul was diagnosed and not long after Donnie was born. I remember the scene. Joni, Paul, and I were sitting on our old couch. Dad was standing in the living room. He had cardboard boxes and a bunch of paper bags. Our parents were yelling at each other like crazy, fighting big time. Mom was throwing clothes out of the bedroom, and they kept landing in the same pile. I remember thinking, *Mom should be a basketball star. She is really good.* Dad would fill up a bag or box, take it outside, then come back in for another bag or box. He packed it all up and left. That's the last time we ever saw him or ever heard from him.

Later, Mom told me stories about how my dad used to love to take me to the park with him when I was a baby. He used me to pick up girls. He did that until I came home with him and said, "Mama, you should have seen the lady daddy was talking to at the park."

I have no feelings toward him at all. I never knew him. When I was young, though, I hated him.

SINGLE

MOM WAS ON HER OWN AFTER DAD LEFT. She had relatives but didn't rely on them even though I come from strong people. My uncle was in World War II. Most of the men in my family were military. One of my uncles has a square named after him in Auburn, Massachusetts. He was in the Marines, and he got killed during the capture of Tinian in the Northern Mariana Islands. My mom always said it was Guadalcanal, but I read the square down in Auburn, and it says he was killed in 1943 on the Island of Tinian. He was a Lance Corporal in the Marines and got shot right in the forehead. He was my father's only brother. All the other male relatives on my father's side of the family, three in-laws, got killed in a boating accident. They were duck hunting in the late '50s and they were out in a flat-bottomed boat. The boat capsized. All three died that day. It was around October so the pond was icy. I have an aunt, and she was in charge of the American Red Cross for the East Coast.

On my mom's side, my Uncle Luis got captured by the Germans. He was one of the lucky ones. Germans killed a bunch of general infantrymen at Normandy. They got Luis and marched him to a prisoner of war camp. Well, he looked around and didn't like what he saw. He took off running and the Germans shot after him. A portion of his leg got ripped up from the barbed wire, but he made it through and kept running and running. He finally he got in with some team of guerilla fighters who got him back to the American lines. He was close to being a POW, and he knew he wouldn't have survived in that camp.

My Uncle Jake down in Washington worked for the State Department. He was in the Office of Strategic Services (OAS), a precursor to the Central Intelligence Agency (CIA). Another uncle was in Bataan. He got captured in Bataan and spent the whole war in a Japanese POW camp. He and this other prisoner (both of them were mathematicians by trade) worked out this formula for a thermal device while they were prisoners. When they were free and back home safe, they got a patent. That uncle became a multi-millionaire.

My Uncle Jack was in the Air Force, and he had some awesome photographs of USA planes burning Germany. After Germany surrendered, he went to Japan, and he took really good photographs of the firestorms after the bombings in Tokyo.

Like her brothers, Mom was tough. She did the best she could for us. Mom never dated. She was a serious Catholic and refused to date after Dad left. She never sought a divorce. She went on ADC, which is Aid for Dependent Children. She didn't get very much, maybe $90 a month. This was long before food stamps. Out of that $90 came rent, utilities, groceries, clothes, and anything else we needed. At the beginning of the month, we'd do okay, but toward the end of the month we were broke. She couldn't work. There were no daycares in the early '50s. She had four young children and Paul needed so much care.

One time I wanted to treat her to a cup of coffee in bed. I remembered, *Mom puts a lot of stuff in it,* so I put some of everything in the refrigerator in it. I brought her cup to her and said, "Mom, I made you a cup of coffee."

She said, "Oh, how sweet." She was still in bed. She took one sip out of it and flew out of that bed, ran to the bathroom, and puked her guts out.

My sister says that story is hers. I tell her, "No, I distinctly remember the ass-whooping I got."

Mom was tuned in to spirits. When I was four or so, Mom and I were going down the hall toward the cellar to get a can of heating oil so the stove could be on all night. She was carrying me. As we went down the stairs, I looked up to see this white glow in the air. It was shining really bright. I said, "Mom! Look at the flying rat!" She looked up and this thing went right by us. You could have reached up and touched it. It went right by us, down the corner, and down into the cellar. I asked, "What was that? What was that?"

She didn't even want to talk about it. She said, "Ah, never mind. Never mind about that. We aren't going to talk about that. Let's just put an extra blanket on your bed tonight."

It was a glow about the size of a basketball. It went right through the cellar door. There was no way my mom was going down into the cellar after that. I have no idea what it was. I've seen so many things in my life, I'd have to say that it was something definitely evil. I don't let the color *white* fool me in my assessment of the thing. It was totally evil. I know my mom felt it because she wouldn't go downstairs to get the heating oil. So, we had a cold night that night. We froze.

She taught us to be independent. That's one thing I thank her for. Once, when I was really young, I said, "Mom, I'm hungry."

She said, "Well, you know where the stove is. Just don't burn the house down."

I had to stand on a milk crate so I could see the top of the stove. And I cooked. I cooked breakfast for myself, Joni, and Paul. Also, we had to do our own laundry. She had an old-time ringer-type washer. We'd twist heavy wet clothes through that contraption and hang them all out on the clothesline. I never could get along with an iron though. Every white shirt I've ever owned has had burn marks on it.

Mom used to write about us kids every couple of months, mostly the mischief we got into, and send her stories to the *Saturday Evening Post.* She called her articles, "My four little Indians." She was tough on us, but she loved us.

I remember one of the worst spankings I ever got in my life. My mom bought everything in commodities, as in 100-pound sacks of flour, sugar, cereal, rice, whatever she could get, to save money. It was pouring rain out and I wanted to play with my truck. I had a new truck and it's not very often you get a new truck. I poured sugar and flour and cereal on the floor, and I made a big mountain in the middle for my truck to drive over. She was so mad about how I wasted food that she spanked me with a razor strap, the kind they use to sharpen single-edged razors in barber shops. One day, I got fed up with that strap and burned it. Then somehow she got a piano key, which is the big wooden key covered with felt. She used that till she broke it on me. After that, when I was going to get a spanking, she'd say, "You're going to get a really bad spanking, but first I want you to go down to the store. Walk down to the store and get me this and get me that. On your way back, pick out a switch, and it better be a good one because if it breaks before I'm done, you're going to go out and get a new one, and we're going to start all over again." I learned to get the thick switches.

Any time we were bad, we got spanked. There was one point where she'd spank me every week, every Friday night. She'd say, "This is for the stuff you thought you got away with." Every Friday night. I remember thinking, *Man, she's got to have cameras or something hidden. How does she know all this?*

Mom was a good cook. She could scrape up a meal out of nothing. We would have ketchup sandwiches for dinner because we didn't have money to buy sandwich meat, but we always had bread. She'd go to the day-old store and buy a bunch of bread at a nickel a loaf and then freeze it. She tried to freeze milk but it never thawed out right. It separated and it was nasty. We drank a lot of Kool-Aid. She made Golumpkis and I would always help her. Basically, Golumpkis are stuffed cabbage. We took hamburger meat and mixed in eggs and crackers and rice. We rolled it into little balls and put the balls in leaves of cabbage. We packaged them up and tied them together with string. We got a big pot boiling with water. We dropped big chunks of potatoes, carrots, cabbage, and the Golumpkis into the pot, and they boiled for about 45 minutes. They were really good. We'd make so many we'd have them three nights in a row for dinner.

Mom had her own recipe for potato pancakes, and to this day I've never had potato pancakes as good as she made them. I kind of remember her recipe, so I make them now, and they're very close to hers, but she had her little tricks. One trick was to put baking soda in the mix and also grate an onion to add a little bit of flavor. That all goes with a couple of eggs and some garlic powder. You mix it all up then pour them into a hot oiled skillet or oiled hot plate. I can eat a half dozen at a time. You've got to let them cook. They don't bubble like regular pancakes. You've got to let them cook for a while, and then you flip them over. Once they're brown on one side, that side is done. Then you flip them and time them so both sides are browned. Set them off and get the next batch going.

TORNADO

STRANGE THINGS HAPPENED DURING MY CHILDHOOD. In 1953, a tornado went right over our house. It hit hard at Great Brook Valley in Worcester. The storm is in the *Book of Lists* because it killed so many people—90 dead and over 500 injured. We lived in the housing projects there in the Valley.

I was only six years old when it happened, but I remember it vividly. I remember playing outside. A city bus rolled by, and it was packed with people, standing room only, going into Worcester. Then rain came down all of a sudden. We were playing on the grass on what had been a nice day out when hail about the size of golf balls started pelting us. Mom got us in the house. The living room, kitchen, and dining room were all together on the first floor, and stairs went up to the bedrooms. We kids sat at the table playing with clothespins, thinking it was just a bad thunderstorm, when the picture window in the living room blew out.

Mom ran us all into the closest closet, but then she changed her mind. She stuffed us under the kitchen sink. She was only able to get her head and shoulders in, and I had my head sticking out from under Mom's arm so I could see. I watched the whole thing.

The kitchen table went airborne. It was like two invisible people picked it up, turned it sideways, and threw it. Out the window it went. We had a big, old, heavy 1940s couch. That thing was bouncing up and down about a foot high in the air. There was a bookcase full of books on the wall, and all I can say is that it became fluid. It slid down the wall and into the middle of the room and spun around a mile a minute. Books flew out of it and slashed *through* the ceiling.

At some point, we got hit with a big bottle and my head was split open, badly. I noticed my mom's ankle was pumping blood out. When the storm calmed down, she told me to go upstairs to get some sheets and Ibuprofen. Something had cut an artery in her ankle. I went to the steps, and all the doors from the bedrooms upstairs were on the stairway. I had to hold the bannister to pull myself up over all the debris. I remember going into the bathroom and looking out the little window there. We had the last brick unit, and behind us were all these wooden houses. There was nothing out there but piles of kindling. Every one of them was destroyed. Every one of them. They were Lincoln Logs.

Nobody knew what had happened. A neighbor came over, and Mom asked her what happened. The neighbor thought that the Russians had nuked us. She said, "I think Russians dropped a bomb on us." It made sense for a couple of reasons. First off, tornadoes in Massachusetts were unheard of. Second, the amount of damage was huge. It was total devastation. The tornado was a Category 4.

Mom was right; we were safer under the sink. That closet where she originally wanted to put us was cut in half by a dining room chair.

Mom didn't drive, so the neighbor drove us toward the hospital. The tornado hit about maybe five to ten minutes after that city bus had gone by. On our way to the hospital, we saw the bus, and it was like a soda pop can that somebody turned on its side and stepped on it right in its middle. I'll never forget that as long as I live. Body parts were like raw hamburger coming out the windows. Everybody in the bus was dead.

We saw cars stacked four and five on top of each other and the people in the top cars were yelling, "Help! Get us down! Get us down!"

A friend of my mom's was in an apartment house, and when the tornado hit she just stood in the corner, covered her eyes up, and started praying, "Jesus, please help me." When it was over, the only thing left of that whole apartment house was that corner and her. She didn't have a scratch on her. She was on the second floor and that was all that was left of the whole entire apartment complex. There were probably twenty or more apartments. Her corner was the only thing left. The tornado was almost a half a mile wide and it cut a swathe right down the middle of the Valley.

Another friend of my mom's was out walking his newborn baby in his stroller and had no idea, of course, that a tornado was coming. When we saw the man, his eyes were all puckered and black from all the stuff that he'd gotten hit with. His baby was impaled on a limb on a tree. Killed. Another lady's freezer lifted off the ground and attacked her. She fell on the ground, and the freezer landed on her. It trapped her and cut her legs off. Mom knew quite a few people who got hurt or killed.

14

The people didn't know what it was, so they were easy targets. Yes, it was just a brutal, horrible, horrible experience.

I remember that when we got to the hospital in Worcester, they were treating people on the lawn. There wasn't even room to get people in the hospital. They brought me right in because I was a child and I was covered with blood. I walked down the corridor and there were people lying on both sides there and writhing in pain. A nurse took me into a room. I don't remember anything after that. I know they stitched up my head. I got a good L-shaped scar to prove it.

Our house was totally lost, so we lived at this housing thing set up for all the people who became homeless because of the tornado. It was the third worst tornado in the history of the country.

PAUL

I HATED MY DAD. I hated him because my brother Paul was so sick, and Dad never made the thirteen-minute drive to see Paul. My dad lived in Auburn, Massachusetts, and we lived in Worcester. I think the worst is that my dad's folks would come up and see my brother, and I knew my dad was in touch with his folks. He knew what was happening, but not once when Paul was sick did my dad ever send him a card or call him up on the phone or come to see him. He had no communication with us for the rest of our lives. He just left. He never held his dying son. And I hated him for it. I kept thinking, *What kind of a man is that?*

I have a picture I keep in my car of the last day that Paul was alive. It's of Paul, Mom, and me sitting there on the hospital bed. The doctors had him on what they called the "24-hour list." They made me leave after they took the picture and about two hours later, my mom came home and her eyes were all red. I said, "Paul?"

She said, "Yes, he passed away."

That was 1959. I was twelve.

For some reason I asked her, "Did he say anything before he died?"

She said, "Yes, he said the most amazing thing."

"What did he say?" I asked.

What she told me made quite an impression on me, but I was angry at God all my life. I cursed Him. I always detested Him because He came and got my brother. I couldn't understand why He would take a little boy, nine years old, my baby brother.

FLAGPOLE

TROUBLE HAS FOLLOWED ME ALL MY LIFE. We had a flagpole in our backyard. We kids would grab a hold of it and spin around and around. One day, we were doing that, and I thought the kid behind me gave me a hard noogie on the head. I turned around ready to fight him and saw my sister trying to lift up this 25-pound brass eagle that had fallen off the top of the pole. She said, "He didn't hit you. This did."

I looked at that and I felt my head. My hand came away all bloody. I went into the house and ran up the stairs. I yelled, "Mom! Mom! I'm gonna die! I'm gonna die!"

She said, "What's the matter?"

I said, "I got hit in the head with an eagle!"

She said, "What do you mean you got hit in the head with an eagle?"

I said, "From the flagpole."

My sister came in with that eagle. Mom said, "Oh, my God." She called a taxi and took me straight to the hospital.

They took me right in and did X-rays of my head. The doctor came out and said, "You don't have anything to worry about. He's got a hard head." They gave me a tetanus shot and some other kind of shot. They told Mom to watch me all night, which she did. It's funny how that happened. It turned out the bolt holding the eagle on the pole had rusted right through. From that distance (25 feet at least), if that eagle had come down any other way or hit me with its wing, which ended in a point, it would have sliced right through me. Any one of those edges would have made the injury much more serious. Mom kind of flipped out a little bit. That was the same summer after Paul died.

BREAKDOWN

MOM HAD HER FIRST PSYCHOTIC BREAKDOWN ABOUT TWO YEARS LATER. Mom's mother died, and that triggered the first of many psychotic episodes. She went off big time on my sister Joni. She was screaming and throwing stuff. I don't know why, but she always turned on my sister during those breakdowns. This time, Joni locked herself in the bathroom, and my mom tried to break the door down to get to her. Mom was so strong that the door started to break. Mom screamed over and over, "I'm going to kill you! I'm going to kill you!"

I was about fourteen at the time, so I was strong, too. I grabbed Mom and said, "Mom, I'm sorry, but I've got to do this. I'm not going to let you hurt Joni." It was awful because I knew I was hurting her, and I loved her.

She yelled, "Let me go! Let me go! She deserves it!"

I said, "No, she doesn't, Mom. It's all in your head. Calm down. Calm down, Mom."

She got madder and madder. She was *screaming*. My friend Kenny was there, and he ran down to his apartment and got his mom Wanda. She came up and called the police department. She told us kids to get out, but I didn't let Mom go until the police arrived. None of us left our mother. We stood there and watched the police take her out of our apartment. She was in a straitjacket and strapped down to the stretcher. We were scared. She had had a total nervous breakdown and none of us really understood what was happening.

We had a house full of furniture, and we had all kinds of possessions accumulated, but when Mom went into psychiatric care that first time, my "lovely" aunts and uncles came into our home and cleaned it out. They were really upset because Mom had some porcelain dolls that belonged to my grandmother. Grandmother had lived with us while she collected those porcelain dolls. They were little George Washington ones, little figurines made to look like that era. She had quite a collection, and when she died she had left all that to my mom. She left a coin collection to us kids. All my aunts and uncles were really upset about it, and they went in and cleaned everything out. They took everything for themselves. They took our stuff, but they wouldn't take us kids in.

Mom was institutionalized for about a year and a half. At first they put Joni, Donnie, and me in a foster home. There was a lot of abuse there. The lady had eleven or twelve foster kids. I came home from school one day, and when I walked in everybody got real quiet. I said, "Hey, what's going on? Where's my brother Donnie?" Joni was sitting there silent and no one would tell me anything. I asked again, "Where is Donnie?" One of the kid's said that Greg, the lady's boyfriend, had him downstairs. So, I went down to the cellar. They were there. Greg had his shirtsleeves rolled back and fist out; he was ready to punch Donnie. I grabbed his arm and spun him around. Then I grabbed my brother, and I said, "If you ever lay a hand on my brother, I'll kill you. I'll kill you dead."

He said, "He wet the bed."

I said, "He has a bladder problem. He has a small bladder, and he can't help it. He doesn't like wetting the bed, but he can't help it. He is a little kid."

I was fourteen or fifteen and big. I've been six feet tall since I was twelve. I worked out with weights. I was a scrapper, and I loved to fight. I guess the guy new it because he backed off.

The next night when I got back to that house Donnie and Joni were gone. Nobody would tell me what happened to them. Finally, the lady said, "They complained about me."

I said, "Well, you know, you get what you deserve."

Joni and Donnie were in grade school, so I didn't know what they were up to during the day. They told me later that when they got off the school bus, they ran down the road and into town where they found the caseworker's office. I guess they made that decision on the ride home; there was no way to let me know. They told the caseworker they wouldn't go back to the lady and her boyfriend. They told about the abuse. The caseworker put them in Saint Anne's orphanage, but I stayed behind at the foster house. I guess social services figured I could take care of myself.

At that house we all suffered physical abuse and neglect. I lost a lot of weight there because the lady never fed me. This lady didn't work, she drove a Cadillac, and she got X number of dollars every month for each one of the foster kids. She was making a living like that.

I didn't say anything to anyone, but my guidance counselor in high school somehow figured it out. He got me a job in the cafeteria so I could eat. I had breakfast, and then I had coffee breaks at 10:00 and at 1:30. It was a trade school, and that's where I started learning plumbing and electrical. My guidance counselor turned in a complaint with social services, and the lady got investigated again.

Thankfully, about that same time, my mom got out of the hospital. Social services set her up with an apartment on Main Street in Worcester. They let me go live with her first. Joni was at the orphanage, and my brother Donnie was in reform school. He acted out. He was a real juvenile delinquent from a very young age. After about two months, they let Joni move in with Mom and me. Donnie moved in after he was released from reform school.

PYROMANIA

I WASN'T A DELINQUENT. That being said, I was for sure a hellraiser and a pyromaniac. I've always loved fire. They used to show us movies in school. One day the teacher showed us a movie about a satellite. We watched the satellite light up, and I decided I was going to build myself a rocket. There at school, I got some tin metal pieces as big around as cans. When I got home, I found a box of matchbooks. I found some gasoline and I got a Bunsen burner going. I took all the match tips off and put them in a quart jar. That jar was packed solid with heads of matches. That's a LOT of matches. It took ripping up book after book to do that. After I put the heads in the jar, I was sitting on the back porch with my legs crossed. The jar sat right in front of me next to my Bunsen burner. The first thing I did was pour the gasoline from a glass jug right into a Styrofoam cup over the Bunsen burner. I was going to heat it up. What I didn't realize is that when you put gasoline in a Styrofoam cup it dissolves. I spilled the cup and the whole jar of matchbooks ignited. A blue flame shot straight up like a rocket flare and hit the ceiling and made a flaming dome over me. The flame was all around me and completely covering the porch but not touching me. Mom happened to look out the window and see it. She hurried and dragged a 100-pound sack of sugar out onto the porch and poured it over the flames. She put the fire out. Once she made sure I wasn't burned, she lit a new fire on my bottom. I messed up when I said, "But Mom, *you* gave me the chemistry set."

I was fascinated by explosions. A lot of times, my best friend Kenny, who was also poor, and I got cheap airplanes from the used book and toy store. They were supposed to still fly but they never did. The engines never worked. We rigged them up with firecrackers and long fuses. We got them going and watched as his flew one way and mine flew the other. Sometimes they got close to crashing into each other. Once the fuse burned out, the planes blew up in the air.

DAREDEVIL

WE WERE ROUNDERS THERE IN WORCESTER. Even when we lived out in the country, we pushed our luck. Mom rented a little house where two country roads met, outside of the city limits of Worcester. I walked everywhere even when I was really young. I had a fishing routine. I got up before the sun and made myself breakfast. I had a can of worms I'd dug the day before, my fishing rod, a little tackle box, and I always had a big canteen for water. I walked eight miles to Lake Quinsigamond to a side dirt pond. It was wide and round, and you couldn't even see the bottom. I liked fishing there because I always got bites. I caught lots of big bluegill and crappie. One day I cast into it, and my big bobber sank underwater right away. I started reeling and realized it was a BIG fish. I caught a huge bass—he was at least seven pounds—in that dark muddy little hole.

About a mile up the road one of my uncles lived with his wife and my cousin on their dairy farm. My cousin and I used to hang out. My uncle had an old empty milk truck. Well, my cousin and I knew how to drive super young and we liked rough adventures, so it made sense that we do something with that old milk truck. We covered the inside of the belly with mats and mattresses and blankets. We drove way out into the woods where there were ditches and hills. One of us would drive and the other would get inside the belly of the truck. We'd flip over and over and roll, but we never got hurt. Sometimes it got stuck on its side, so we'd climb out and set it up right again. I think we were about eleven years old. We were tough. I was fearless. I remember getting into a fight with a seventeen-year-old kid who had a broken arm. He was twice as big as I was and much stronger. Not far into the fight, he was whooping me. He kept trying to get me to say "uncle" and I wouldn't do it. The more he told me, the more I refused, and the more he beat me up. He'd think I was knocked out, and I'd pop back up again and square off. Finally, he got scared and ran. Other friends of mine were there. One said, "That guy whooped you, but you won the fight. He was scared to death of you." That's how it rolled. All the time.

CAPE COD

WE DID FUN STUFF AS A FAMILY, TOO. When I was a kid, we used to go to Cape Cod quite a bit. My uncles used to come up every now and then. They'd grab all of us kids or one or two of us and take us to the Cape. We'd fish and hunt for snails and clams. I'd get a whole bunch and bring them home. Mom would cook them up and eat them. I never caught a fish. I caught oysters. I'd fill up big buckets. It wasn't restricted like it is now. Now they have agents dressed in civilian clothes. They stand at all the walls, watching anyone who has a bucket. It's strict. You can fish, but you've got to have a license.

Say you and your husband are out there and you each have a clamming license. Each one of you is allowed eight quarts of clams or oysters. Nothing more. Say your husband is a lot faster. He fills his bucket up and decides to give you a hand. That's what they are watching for. The minute they see him pick up a clam and drop it in your bucket, they come in on you and revoke your licenses. You're illegal because your husband's put clams in your bucket. They could confiscate his load and your load and give you a ticket for about $500. You can lose your license for the rest of the year.

It happened to a friend of mine. His bucket was full and his wife's had little. He dug up a bunch and carried them in his T-shirt. He brought them over and poured them in her bucket. No sooner did he do that than fish and game officers came over. They said, "You took clams you gathered from the beach and put them in her bucket. You're cooperating with us, so we aren't going to remove your rights, but we're taking your licenses for the rest of the year."

It's all inland where you do it. Marshes. I'm trying to find somebody who's gone down there lately and knows where the good places are. I'll mark them off on a map. That's where I'll go. I love clams. I hope to go down there. When I do go, I'll follow the rules.

WOODS

I HAD A LOT OF FREEDOM. From the time we were seven or so years old, neighborhood kids and I camped out in the woods all summer. Children don't have that kind of independence anymore. There are too many perverts around. Back in those days we had a whole little clique of us—probably eight to ten boys and maybe a dozen girls—and we'd all go camping together. The first thing we did in the woods was to find us a club spot. We rummaged around and brought or found stuff to sit on, like old lawn chairs, blankets, logs, and mattresses, and we made a fire pit. We made our own bows and arrows, too, and they were really good. We glued the feathers to the ends and made arrowheads out of bottle caps. We folded the caps around the tips of the twigs and filed them till they were sharp enough to stick into the trees. We hunted rabbits and squirrels and taught ourselves how to skin them, clean them, and cook them over the campfire. Someone always kept the campfire going.

We all brought backpacks from home filled with whatever we thought may be useful. It was a blast. We went to Bell Pond and Lake Quinsigamond to fish and swim. We played lots of games. There was a field near the woods, and out there we played softball and stickball. It was fun just camping out, having fun, and telling stories. We only went home when we ran out of food. We camped out for two or three weeks at a time. The parents knew where we were, and we walked there, so I guess we were only about three or four miles from the neighborhood.

Everybody was poor, so we pooled our money together and every week bought a bunch of hotdogs and eggs, bacon, and coffee. I was drinking coffee from the time I could pour it into a cup. It was a big deal to the other kids. When we camped, they all wanted coffee. A lot of them weren't allowed to drink it at home. I brought cream and sugar at first and then bull's milk later. It's evaporated milk in a can. My grandmother always called it bull's milk and the name stuck with me. Usually, it is with the baking supplies at the grocery store.

One day a couple of years ago, I was looking for it, and it wasn't there. I asked this young girl, "Do you know where the bull's milk is?" This was here in New Hampshire, where I live now. She didn't blink an eye.

She said, "Yes, it's over in aisle [so-and-so]," and then it dawned on me that most twenty-year-old girls wouldn't call it that.

I said, "I'm glad to see that you know what bull's milk is."

She said, "Well, yes, my grandmother, that's what she called it."

I said, "My grandmother, that's what she called it, too."

But it blew me away that a young girl knew it. Older clerks will say, "Yes, the canned milk is over there." They know exactly what I'm talking about because back in the '40s and the '50s, that was what that generation called canned milk—*bull's milk*.

One summer we had a clubhouse that was an old watchtower with iron bars in the windows. We camped out in there, which was great in the rain. We closed the gates and made it a little fortress. The government tore ours down many years later, but there's another in the area that's 56 feet tall. It's called Bancroft Tower, after the politician George Bancroft. In my childhood the towers were abandoned. If you were looking on a map, a farm was at the top and had a barn, a haystack, and corrals for a bunch of cows. The house was to the right, and our club spot with the tower was in the woods below a little drop-off, south of the farm.

One day, we were out exploring in the woods there and found a five-gallon bucket of pitch. My cousin was with me. He said, "What do you want to do with this pitch?"

I said, "Hey, I've got an idea. Let's make fire arrows like in the movies." We dipped some arrows in the black tar. Then we wrapped and tied cloth around the tips and dipped them in the pitch again. We had an old mattress and used it for target practice and loved watching it burn.

We always had a campfire going. We made a bunch of those fire arrows. We got bored with the mattress so we started shooting the arrows straight up into the air. We did that for a good while until all of a sudden we heard walkie-talkies and yelling and then sirens coming from the farm.

We wondered what was going on, so we crawled up to the top of the hill. The first thing we saw were firetrucks roaring onto the property. Policemen were running around with their guns out saying, "Where are they coming from? Where are they coming from?" We looked and a haystack was on fire, and a shed roof was on fire with fire arrows sticking in it. The corral was on fire. The house was on fire. It was bad. The police and firemen were running around trying to figure out where the arrows were coming from. We scrambled down the hill, and I said, "Man, I'm going home. I'm going home. I think you better go around the other way and walk down the road like you were somewhere else." I ran all the way home, and my uncle was there waiting for me. He knew it was his son and me who caused the fire. I feel like we were innocent because we didn't think anything of shooting those arrows until they came down and started the fires. He paddled my butt big time, but he didn't turn me in to the police. When he got done, Mom paddled my butt even worse. Then my uncle went home and paddled his son's butt. We weren't allowed to play together ever again. We didn't hang out until we were eighteen or nineteen years old when we saw each other at a town dance.

We camping kids always used to light forest fires and then put them out. We played "forest service." First, we started a little fire. Then we pretended to be TV reporters and said, "Okay, we just got here on the scene," and sayings like that. Others were the firefighters. They got shovels and cut in the fire lines, made the backfires, and then put them all out. Only one time did a fire get away from me in the woods. The fire department showed up, and I helped put the flames out. I think they knew I started it, but I didn't cop to it. I was old for my age, if you consider I was eight or nine then. I was a fire maniac. I still like fire.

I camped all the way through my teens. Kenny camped with me. He was one of the best friends I ever had. I met him when we moved to Providence Street and he lived on the top floor. It was inevitable that we would finally lock horns. The whole block was tenement houses like ours, and we shared a huge backyard. One day Kenny and I got out in the backyard, and we started fighting. We were going at it. We were both around twelve or thirteen years old, and we were really scraping. Our shirts were torn off. We were all dirty and bloody. People were cheering at first, but after about 30 minutes they started yelling to each other, "Somebody's got to stop them. They're killing each other." We were on our knees, and he hit me, boom, in the head. I came back, and it was my turn. I hit him, boom, and then he got me back. We traded punches. Finally, after about ten minutes of that, we knew we couldn't knock each other out, so we just looked at each other and started laughing. We hugged and became best friends after that. He was one of the best friends I ever had. His mom's boyfriend owned a piece of land out in Milford that was right on a lake. There was an island. We worked part-time all during the school year to save up so we could camp on that island all summer. I worked three different jobs. I gave Mom the first half of my pay to help her out. I took a quarter for myself to buy clothes and school supplies and put the other quarter in the bank. Mom could go into the bank account for me, so about every week of the summer she got money out, bought us groceries, and brought them to our camp. Sometimes Kenny's mom stopped at Coney Island Hot Dogs and brought us out these foot-long hot dogs and French fries.

We weren't alone. Kenny had this little Pomeranian dog, a little bitty dog. We were exploring down a backroad one day until it ended at a big estate. The place had a big barn and fence. In the distance, we saw a horse. Well, the gate was open and there was nobody around, so I thought, *Let's have a look at that.*

Kenny's dog also saw. He said, "Yip, yip, yip, yip, yip," and tore off barking down the pasture. He got close and that horse said, "WOOF!" It was a Harlequin Great Dane. That little dog shot by us, her tail between her legs, peeing the whole time. That Pomeranian yipped and peed and ran back toward the camp. Kenny and I both looked at each other and said, "I'm not going near that dog." We ran back to camp, too.

At night we took the boat out into the lake. One time we camped on the island on Halloween weekend. We had a battery-operated radio, so we played the rock and roll station. That night the fog was about four feet high off the lake. We were just floating around when we heard a huge splash. It was about midnight, so we figured we'd better get the motor started. Kenny said, "Let's get to shore."

Well, he tried to start the motor and it stalled. The radio station was building up to a climax and then it happened. The D.J. played "Monster Mash." It spooked us big time. Kenny finally got the motor going and when we finally made it back to shore, we jumped into the tent and didn't come out until daylight.

MOTORCYCLE

I'VE ALWAYS LOVED MOTORCYCLES. When I was a little kid—about eight or nine years old—one of the neighbors had a big old Harley. He took me for a ride on it, and I just fell in love with motorcycles. I got my first one when I was fourteen years old. It was an old Harley Davidson Chopper, a motor scooter.

What had happened is this young guy down the street had bought it, and he had torn it all down to rebuild. He was in the military and before he had time to do it, he went overseas to Vietnam and got killed. His dad boxed the parts up and sat the stuff in his garage for a long time. Finally, he decided to get rid of it. Kenny heard about it. The man wanted $25 for it, so Kenny and I split the cost and brought him $25. It was a motor scooter with a big flathead engine. The man gave us a box and paper bags full of parts. In the box was a little manual to figure out how to put it back together. Kenny's dad was a machinist, so he showed us how to make gaskets. Kenny and I figured it out and put the bike together.

Kenny wanted to ride the bike first because he found it. It was a kickstart bike, and one of the things we didn't know about was the safety switch, so we didn't wire it up when we assembled the bike. Kenny got up in the seat. He kicked the bike and started it up. Well, he was wearing bagging pants and the kicker went right inside his pants. The throttle was stuck open, so the bike was going around and around hysterically while Kenny was hopping on one foot and screaming, "Shut it off! Shut it off!" If we'd installed that safety switch he'd have been able to knock off the power.

It was so funny and I was laughing so hard that I fell down on the ground. Two minutes later his dad came out and saw Kenny spinning around. The next thing I knew, his dad was lying down beside me, and we were just laughing our butts off. Finally, the bike stalled out, so Kenny got his pants leg off of it. He told me, "Give me $12.50, and it's all yours. Buy me out."

I did. That was two years before I could get a driver's license, so I used to go out at night and ride it in the dark so police, hopefully, wouldn't see. I found an old motorcycle license plate alongside the freeway, and I put that on the back of the bike. I peeled a sticker off something else and put it on the plate. I'm amazed I never got pulled over driving it. I was illegal as all get out. That's what got me started on Harleys. I got into the habit of buying basket cases, bikes that were trashed up and totally torn apart. I rebuilt each one. I liked that because I got to know the bikes. Also, once you redo a bike that way, it's your design. I was really into it.

The only time it wrecked was when a friend of mine, one of the tough guys, asked if he could ride it. I said, "Be careful on it."

He said, "I know what I'm doing." Well, he took off around the corner and I heard a crash. Then he came running back, pushing the bike. He'd popped a wheelie and hit a car that was parked right in front of him.

I rode that bike until I was seventeen or eighteen. Once I was legal, I'd ride during the day and fill it up on my last ride home. My little brother Donnie used to sneak over to my bed at night and steal the keys out of my pants pocket. Well, I'd wake up the next day and take my bike out, and it would run out of gas. He would drain all the gas out of it. So, I set a trap for him one night. I kept Hershey's chocolate bars by my bed all the time. Well, I bought a bar of Ex-lax and switched the wrappers. I laid that wrapped Ex-lax there on the table beside my bed. It lay there about a week. Finally, one night I heard Donnie crawl across the floor. He had a weird laugh, like, "Hep, hep, hep, hep. Hep, hep, hep." I heard him chuckling. Then I saw his hand reach up and grab that bar. I heard him open it up and start eating it. I thought, *Yep, we'll see what happens.* About an hour later, he started going out of the bedroom to get glasses of water. More water and more water. Then he was going to the bathroom really quick. He didn't learn a lesson from it. The very next night, he was looking for my keys again.

EDUCATION

I LIKED LEARNING. I enjoyed my time at Worcester Boys Trade High School, especially the teachers and the guidance counselor who got me the job in the cafeteria. I had a part-time summer job as a plumber's helper. But, after about three years I decided I didn't want to make my living by cleaning up people's messy toilets. What really helped me figure that out was when I went into a chicken slaughterhouse to replace a toilet. The toilet had a heavy old box up above with the toilet down below, and I had to put a whole new system in. That smell in the poultry place got to me. I gagged the whole time I worked on that toilet, and for about two weeks I burped up that smell from the place. I thought, *There's got to be a better way to make a living.* I was studying electrical at the same time. Both sets of skills have come in handy over the years. I've gotten a lot of good jobs because I have the ability do plumbing *and* electrical work.

We were doing okay, but then my mom got sick again. No one ever healed her. Things would be good for a while, and then she'd need to be institutionalized again. Two months shy of my graduation from the trade school, Mom cracked again. The social workers said I was old enough to stay home, but Donnie and Joni would have to go back into the orphanage. I said, "No. I will take care of them."

The social worker said, "You can't. You are in school. Someone has to be home all the time."

I said, "Then I'll quit school and take care of them."

The social worker argued, "You can't do that. If you quit school, you'll have to get a job."

I said, "Wait a minute now, make up your mind. You just got done telling me that there's got to be somebody at home, but if I'm working, I'm not going to be home."

He said, "Well, you need to get a job."

I quit eight weeks shy of graduation. It was worth it because they didn't split up our house again. I took care of Donnie and Joni. I'd get Mom's welfare check, ride my bike to Worcester State Hospital and have her sign it, and then I could go grocery shopping. If Joni and Donnie went with me, we hitchhiked. Back then hitchhiking was safe. I didn't graduate from high school.

Mom was in about eight months that time. When she came home, she was very spaced out. They had her on all kinds of medicine and gave her shock treatments. It wasn't pretty. She would do weird stuff like just stand in the kitchen and stare into space. If we tried to talk to her, she didn't hear us. She was in her own world. There was no snapping her out of it. She was usually home for six to eight months, and then she'd be sick again and be institutionalized for six to eight months. Life just alternated between one and the other. We were glad she was home, though.

In the meantime, I had quite a few different jobs and was going to college classes. I didn't have a high school diploma, but Clark University let me study agriculture. I didn't enroll. I just sat in classes. Local kids here and there did the same. We could even take the tests, but we weren't graded unless we paid tuition. I didn't care about that. I went there to learn. I tried. I did my best. I tried my best.

It was hard because we were poor and life was chaotic. We had no good leadership. Donnie and I fought all the time. First we played like heroes in movies. We'd fight with machetes and sparks would fly off. Jonie would freak out and call up the police. By the time they got there, Donnie I would be sitting on the couch watching TV. We always embarrassed her. She'd say to the cops, "You should have seen them an hour ago! They were killing each other!"

Donnie or I would say, "What are you talking about, Sis?"

RELIGION

MOM DID HER BEST. Even when she was sick, she made us go to church. We went through Holy Communion, Confirmation, and stuff like that, but I really wasn't into it, and it bothered me because the priest talked in Latin. I couldn't understand what he said. I got to the point where I just didn't go to church. Mom gave me a dime every Sunday to turn in for tithing. I acted like I was walking to church, but I went to the corner drugstore. I bought a pop and some penny candies. I stayed there, read comic books for an hour or so, and then I walked back home. She thought I was in church.

Because she was sick, she didn't usually go. After about three months of my sneaking out, Mom got a letter from the church. It said something like, "Your son hasn't been in church. He hasn't been turning in his envelopes and we know how much he usually turns in, so we figure he owes us X amount of money."

Mom said, "You haven't been in church?"

I said, "No."

She said, "What's that about? They want the money that you're supposed to be turning in."

I said, "I'll tell you right now, Mom, I'm never going back to that church because it's not about God. It's about money. You can spank me all you want, but I won't go back to that church."

She let it go.

I completely turned away from God.

WORK

I WORKED A LOT OF JOBS. I worked for a W.T. Grant department store for a while. There was a cafeteria in the store where I washed dishes and bused tables. I worked a lot of jobs and got frustrated sometimes. At Grant I worked hard, really hard. There were supposed to be three guys on my shift, but the restaurant just had me. I was doing three guys' work. I kept telling the manager, "You've got to get me some help here."

His attitude was, "This guy is doing all the work, so why hire anybody else?" I finally got so upset I quit.

Once, I worked in a toy factory making baby carriages. I did the painting. I put the carriages on a conveyor tool that dipped them down into the paint and took them out. After that, I put on designs.

I worked for Shell Oil for a little while and then I worked for United Steel doing sandblasting. United Steel had a heating plant where they heated up metal and dipped it in some kind of oil to make it even harder. I was with United Steel for one year, but they had a layoff.

Right away I went to work for a machine shop. We made these little round things that looked like the tops of big five-gallon milk cans. They had something to do with rockets. It was a government contract and I ran a drill press. My job was to drill holes through those round things. We had to make something like three or four million of them. I was kind of making rockets again, but this time for Cape Canaveral. The machine shop was right above the Worcester Boys Trade School. I made good money, real good money. I think I took home about $60 a week, and that was in the early '60s. Minimum wage was $1.15 an hour, and I was eventually making about $2.50 gross an hour working for the shop. Plus, I got all the overtime I wanted. I liked to work overtime. I wasn't into dating or any of that kind of stuff.

PENNE ANTE

I DIDN'T GO OUT. Even though I was a rambler, I didn't really date in high school or after that. There weren't many girls around, anyway. On weekends, my buddies would come up to my house and we'd play penny ante poker games. We took up a collection and drove my mom up to a store. She got us a couple of cases of beer, snacks, sandwich meat, and bread. We filled the bathtub up with cases of beer, put a block of ice in the tub with cold water, and played penny ante all weekend. Those blocks of ice are hard to find these days. The ones we used were a little bit bigger than a foot thick and wide. We had a ball. We started on Friday evenings and a steady parade of people came through. All the time, though, guys would come in and say, "We're going to have a rumble tonight. Bob, come and help us out." It got to where I didn't want anyone answering the door anymore. They came one after another, after another. I liked fighting, but I wanted to play poker. I'd turn them down and say, "Sorry, can't be any help to you this time."

They fought because they were in gangs, as in, "Our territory is here and your territory is there." People crossed over and caused problems. Worcester is a good size city. Back then, the blacks didn't fight with the whites. Puerto Ricans would. The blacks stayed to themselves. They hung out in the area down by Summer Street. I used to go down there some. I had really good black friends and liked their bar. They had Knickerbocker long neck beers for a nickel. It was made right outside Worcester. I started going in that bar when I was eighteen. I had a phony ID that I made, myself. It was easy, really. I took my driver's license card and used a razor blade to separate where it said, "47." I pulled the seven off and got another number from something that said "41." I glued that on but did it in a way that you couldn't tell. Then I just rubbed a little bit of dirt on it.

I wasn't in a gang. I was just a fighter and had a reputation as a good one. I hung out with a tough crowd. I met most of them through the YMCA. There was a gym down there. We'd work out, boxing. I met a guy at W.T. Grants when I worked there who ran numbers and got fights together. He wanted me to fight in the ring but the money wasn't all that great, just $60 for three rounds.

At Grant's, I stacked 55-gallon drums of soap onto this rack that was about four or five feet high. I'd get down, pick up a drum, and put it on the rack. I lifted about 400 pounds total. I was strong. I've been a strong man all my life. That soap lifting blew the fight guy away. He watched me shadow box at the YMCA and said, "Man, I got to get you in the ring, I can hook you up, man, get you in there."

I said, "What is it paying?"

He said, "Well, it pays $60 if you win."

I said, "I make that working at Grants in a week. Why would I want to go and beat somebody up for that?" (I had no concept of my getting *my* butt whooped.) "It's not worth it," I said. I turned him down, but I was always getting into fights—just not getting paid for them.

BIKER

I WAS A ONE-PERCENTER. I hung out with outlaw motorcycle cults. When I was living in Worcester, Massachusetts, I had friends that were with the Devil's Disciples. That's a big East Coast motorcycle club. I think they've become the Outlaws now. They were warring big time with the Hells Angels back then. I think they're finally at peace, but over the years there was a lot of killing. It was war. I never officially joined them, but I rode with them. I was an associate. I was offered a patch once. There's a certain way you have to turn it down so you don't offend anybody. I turned it down because I got into a fight with somebody who was an enemy, and the next thing I knew all these Disciples jumped in and start stomping this guy. I said, "Wait a minute. This is personal. This is a personal fight. This is not your thing." When you're a biker in a fight, the whole club comes in. That bothered me because this guy and I had known each other since we were young and we saw each other a lot. We had just started to sort it out. It was a personal thing.

One of Devil's Disciples said he would put me up as a *prospect*. How it works is you run prospect for about a year. It's like a probation thing, but there's a lot to it. You're like a slave to those of the club. You have to do anything they ask you to do, and you get all the dirty jobs there are for about one year. They then decide whether you're going to be accepted as a member or not. Back then they used marbles to vote. They had white marbles and they had black marbles. They voted by putting the marbles in a hat, and if you got one black marble you had to be a prospect for a while longer or you were banned. All it took was one person to not want you in, and that was enough because they were all members of the club. It had to be a unanimous vote.

If you turn them down, you have to be very diplomatic so they don't get the idea that you think you're too good to be with them. If they get that idea, you can get hurt bad.

I told them I was honored that they asked me and I was excited to have them as riding buddies, but I just didn't think that I could make that heavy commitment to them. I talked to the brother who hooked me up as a prospect. He had already talked to other club members. They gave him the go-ahead to do that. He offered the patch to me, and I just had to turn it down as diplomatically as I could so I didn't ruffle any feathers. I still liked hanging out with them.

NEW YORK CITY

I MOVED TO NEW YORK CITY. I went from Worcester to New York City, to Greenwich Village. This is crazy. I was just hanging out in the Village in the Square, around 1964, and spotted this guy playing his guitar and singing. I thought, *Man, he can play the guitar all right, but he has a terrible voice.* I walked up to him, introduced myself, and told him I played conga drums. We laughed because I said, "I'm Bob," and he said, "Yeah? My name is Bob, too." We sat there and smoked a joint while he played his music. After he left, my friend Maria came running up and said, "Do you know who that is?"

I said, "Some guy named Bob."

She said, "That's Bob Dylan, and he's going to be famous someday. He is playing a coffee shop tonight."

I said, "Well he'd better not quit his daytime job. He's got a terrible voice."

Maria was Joni's best friend. Still is. She is like a sister to me. She and Joni were hanging out in the early '60s in New York, and I wanted to get away from the gangs in Worcester, so I figured New York would be a cool experience.

When I got to Greenwich Village, I had to get some work. I found an employment agency there. I met with a guy and told him what all I could do. He said, "Well, I've got the perfect job for you."

I started working for a nuclear engineer. Earl Reiback was his name. He liked my work so much that he paid the fees and hired me directly out from under the agency. He invented pieces of luminal art, which were electric color boxes. If you put your stereo on, they reacted. They blinked and they played with the music. Light was the medium and Reiback had the original patent. I called them *luminars*. We made some the size of a whole wall and put one in the Time-Life Building. It was 40 feet wide. We sold one to a nightclub in Rio de Janeiro, but that deal fell through before we could install the piece.

I was the only worker Reiback had. He put chemicals on slides and hit the slides with a laser. My job was to assemble the boxes. I did all the soldering and electrical work. Now and then he'd send me out to round up young ladies who wanted to model. He paid me $25 for every girl I brought in. He paid them $75 to model for an hour. They were naked in front of a black screen. He cast lasers on them and went through a process to somehow capture their movements for the artwork. The schedule was strange, but I liked it. Four days a week, we started at about nine in the morning and worked until midnight. Then we'd go out for dinner. He knew everybody in New York. That was his city.

Reiback started off as a scientist making nuclear weapons. He got tired of it and somehow got into luminal art. He created all the stuff out of his brownstone house in New York City. It was close to Greenwich Village in lower Manhattan. I walked there. I did a lot of walking then. His shop was set up on the third floor. When we finished a big luminar, he had to hire whole crews to disassemble pieces and carry them down. Then we had to reassemble them at installation sites. He was a real easygoing gentleman.

The problem Reiback had was that he waited too long to start manufacturing—five years after he got the patent. So, he had only two years left to manufacture before everybody could start copying his work. He made quite a bit of money, and we got written up in *Time* magazine. I think that was in the summer of 1967.

One time he hired a secretary, a girl named Spanky McFarlane. She was in a music group called Spanky and Our Gang. They were kind of big in the '60s. I'd been working for Reiback for a year, and I knew my way around. She got in the way. The first day she worked there, I walked in, and she asked, "Who are you? What are you doing in here?"

I said, "Who are you?"

She said, "I'm the secretary."

I said, "I'm Bob. I work for Earl."

She said, "Well, let me tell you what you're going to do today."

I said, "No, hold it right there. I don't work for you. I work for Earl. Earl tells me what I'm going to do, not you." She got all mad at me and went to Earl.

Earl said, "No. He works for me. He doesn't work for you. You don't tell him anything. Bob knows what he's doing."

Spanky McFarlane was her stage name. Her real name was Elaine. One of her band members nicknamed her after Spanky McFarland from *The Little Rascals* show. So, she had a band. They were cutting an album and going on *The Ed Sullivan Show*. One of their songs was "Everybody's Talking." It was written by Fred Neil. They sang "Sunday Will Never Be The Same" and "Like to Get to Know You."

Spanky was on the phone all day long talking to her friends about the album, so business calls for Earl couldn't come through. He finally wound up getting rid of her because she was just using his phone and wasting time talking to her friends.

I lived in Greenwich Village on West 15th street. Then I moved to West 12th Street, and later I moved over to East Village for a little while, but I didn't stay very long there. That was the Bowery, which was loaded with drunks and drug addicts. I lived down East 7th Street there, but I moved to the Bronx for a little while and stayed with some friends. It's expensive, so I had a roommate. He was a bass player for a group called The Left Banke. They debuted a song about that time. I can't remember it, but their big hit was *Walk Away Rene.* My roommate George stayed in New York after the band split up. He was going into another band called The Breath of Spring, but they never materialized because the guy who was writing the music was on too much of a needle trip. He started telling the producers what to do and what *he* wanted. They just looked at him and said, "Nah. We are not going to mess with you. Too much other talent out there."

New York was all right. What I didn't like about it is that you could take a shower, then go out and walk around the block and come back dirty again because there was so much smog in the air. I didn't like that I couldn't see the stars at night. I did like the nightlife. The clubs went all night long. I could dance all night. There were discotheques that always piped in music. They were right in Greenwich Village, itself, around Macdougal and Bleecker Street and in that area; there were probably ten of them. The clubs had dance floors, and people would meet and they would dance and hang out. I finally started dating when I moved to New York City. I had a lot of friends there, and girls asked me out all the time. I don't know why. I was wild looking. Still am. My hair was shoulder length and I combed it straight back. I had a beard, which had color back then. My hair was brown, my beard was red, and I wore a mustache, which was blonde. I've always had a ponytail. People ask me, "When was the last time you went to a barber shop?" The last time I remember, I was living in Worcester, I was a kid, and it was 25 cents if you went to the barber college to get a haircut. Before that my mom would put a bowl on my head and cut around it.

The key to the excitement of New York City was that there was so much to do. I remember going down to Coney Island. They had three roller coasters. One was called the *Hurricane*, which wasn't too bad. The next one was called the *Tornado*, and that wasn't too bad. Then they had the *Cyclone*, which was the highest and fastest. I remember I got drunk one day and rode that thing all afternoon. Then the next day I went back, I was sober, and I went at it one time and wanted off! That thing went straight up in the air and topped out, then immediately dropped straight down. It did a complete loop. I was upside-down traveling, and there was so much momentum because the coaster went so high up. The car was flying when the ride ended. I felt like I had to hit the brakes to stop. It was quite a ride.

BACK

I STAYED IN NEW YORK FOR A YEAR. I don't remember why I left, but I think it had something to do with my mom because I went back up to Worcester. Worcester is in the center of Massachusetts. It's halfway between Springfield and Boston. It's a big city, pretty, but with lots of tenement houses. There are some high rises in the middle of town. I hung out there until Mom got better and then I went to California. I just had to get out of Massachusetts. The police really messed up big time and I told them that, too. They were busting pot dealers, but they were ignoring heroin, thinking it would just go away.

I knew better, but I was shooting it up. I started that around 1966. I got started smoking pot, but when the police put the skids on that business, my friends and I couldn't get pot anymore. We wanted something to get high, so somebody said, "Well, try this." Everybody in my socioeconomic group was doing heroin, so I started doing it, but I didn't like it. The first thing is you get a rush from it. You get real hot and you're like that for about an hour, and then you start vomiting. Once you vomit you're high after that for a while and then it wears off, and you've got to get another fix.

When I was high on heroin, I could see things, kind of like I was on an LSD trip. I wasn't addicted automatically. I was never even strung out, but I shot up a lot of stuff just to get high. Then something bad happened. A so-called friend attacked this girl, and she was a sweetheart. I loved her like a little sister. He put her in the hospital. He did a bad thing to her, and she wouldn't tell me who he was. She couldn't live with it, and she wound up killing herself. Well, I found out who had done the bad thing to her, and I went down to see him. The only thing I'll say is he never hurt any girls again. He never hurt anybody else again. I did what had to be done. I wish I had known earlier what he was really like because I would have done what I did long before, and that little girl would still be alive. She was eighteen. He was 30.

After that young lady died, I threw away everything—syringes, eye droppers—everything that had to do with heroin. I trashed it and said to myself, "I'll never touch it again." I kept my promise. I have passed the test because I've had people offer me balloons and I've turned them down cold. I didn't go through withdrawals. To me, that's all a state of mind. I've been able to quit things I was supposedly addicted to and never had any weird sensations like spiders crawling on me. I was strung out, but I was strong enough to overcome it.

In my world, everybody was fighting and doing drugs. I was wild, but I still had a code. My main rule in life has always been and always will be that you don't hurt children, and you don't hurt women. It was getting too crazy in Worcester. I felt, "Well, everybody is moving to California; I might as well try it." Mom was okay with my moving. She was doing better by then. When she said goodbye, she made me promise her that when she died I'd be there for her funeral, and that I would sing a hymn for her, "Amazing Grace."

CALIFORNIA

I TOOK A BUS ALL THE WAY TO CALIFORNIA. I had about $1,000 on me. On Easter Sunday I got off the bus in Los Angeles. I remember thinking, *It was snowing when I left Worcester, and people here are surfing in the ocean.* Once, when I was in Cape Cod, I tried surfing, but I didn't know how to stop and I wiped out. The surfboard came down and cracked me on top of the head and almost knocked me out. I told my friends, "No. That's it. No more surfing for me."

I stayed in North Hollywood with friends for about two weeks. I thought, *I want to see what San Francisco is like.* I lasted ten days in San Francisco and I got out of there. L.A. and San Francisco were too crowded. The air was dirty and, like in New York, I couldn't see the stars at night. There was so much smog and there were so many people. Then I fell in love with Big Sur.

I couldn't drive from San Francisco to Big Sur. I literally walked most of my way there. It was the winter of 1969, a bad winter, and there were major mudslides everywhere. Lots of roads had washed out. I read that Mt. Baldy got over 50 inches of rain in just over one week in January. I was coming up from L.A. through San Luis Obispo. People who were driving were stuck in certain towns because the roads they needed were destroyed. They gave me rides from one washout to the next washout. Otherwise, I hiked. It took me three days to go about a normal six-hour, 300-mile drive. Between rides I camped out in the woods. I had about 25 pounds of dried rice, beans, coffee, and a coffee pot on my back, along with camping gear and my sleeping bag. I went out in the creeks and caught crawdaddies. I picked wild onions and other greens that I could eat. I broke the crawdaddies' tails off them, skinned them, cooked them, and mixed the meat with the rice. I put wild onions and whatever else I could find in the pot to make a good curry. It was really good, actually. I just reached down and grabbed those crawdaddies. They can't sting. They do bite down on the hand, but I just laughed when they bit me. It didn't hurt. I caught nice ones and it never took long. Their tails were about as big as my thumb, so I got some good chunks of meat. With a about 40 or 50 you have a nice little meal going. I set snares up and caught doves. I learned to do all those things during my childhood summers camping in the woods with my buddies.

BIG SUR

I REMEMBER MY FIRST MOMENTS IN BIG SUR. As soon as I got to Big Sur, proper, I was down in the center of town where the post office and general store were. Near them were a restaurant, gas station, and ambulance garage. This guy walked over to me and said, "Hey, you just come up?"

I said, "Yes, just got here."

He said, "You're one of the first people who has gotten through."

I explained how I hiked and hitched through the washouts.

He asked, "Where are you staying?"

I said, "I don't know. I just got here, so I'm looking for a place to stay and looking for a job."

He said, "Well, stay up here at our place."

He and his friends, three other guys, took me in. That day, I got a job at the Lodge—Redwood Lodge. I worked there for the next three years. I started out washing dishes, then I worked at the gas station and managed the bar. I was also a bartender and waiter in there. We had a campground and I was a handyman. I did a little bit of everything.

The gas station was on the TV show *Then Came Bronson*. At the start of one of the episodes, Michael Parks, the guy who played Bronson, rides through the Los Padres National Forest. Well, at one point he pulls into a Phillips 66 service station on his motorcycle, gases it up, and rolls off. That is the lodge where I worked. I was there when he did that, but the TV crew didn't want anyone around.

I met a lot of cool people in Big Sur. A really nice lady was Ms. Price. One of the owners of the lodge, a guy who lived in L.A., was a psychiatrist. Ms. Price was a friend of his, and one day he happened to be up there, and she was with him. He introduced us and told her, "If you need someone to watch over your property, this is your guy right here. He's perfect for you."

Ms. Price was elderly, around 90 years old at that time, and had been a nurse during World War I. She had a house in Big Sur and lived mostly on an estate on 17-Mile Drive between Carmel by the Sea and Monterey.

I was caretaker of her property. The big house near Carmel was actually a mansion on the coast. My job was to watch her property and make sure nobody trespassed. She had problems with her septic tank once, so I had to drain all the water out of it, turn the pump off, and get inside. I shoveled about a foot of mud out, one bucket at a time, by climbing a ladder, dumping the mud, and going back in. Emptying the tank one pail at a time took me almost three full days. I let it dry, then sealed the tank. I also sawed up trees that fell and got rid of all the wood by cutting it into firewood-sized logs. I left it on the side of the road and people grabbed it up.

Working for her was cool because from her yard I saw sea lions, bears, and seals. Some days, if I was lucky, I could sit there, look out over the ocean, and see whales migrating. They weren't that far off, so I got to really look hard at the whales. Ms. Price was old at that time, so she's long since passed on.

I loved Big Sur. I eventually got a bike and loved to get out on the highway. It climbed way up into the mountains, so high up that I could look down and see clouds. That's one of the coolest things I've ever seen in my life: white clouds the size of islands, floating over the sea and the forest, with huge trees that looked like tiny pines poking up through the mist.

CLUB

I HUNG WITH BIKERS IN CALIFORNIA. There were a lot of them in Big Sur, but they weren't all club members. The only clubs that I ever saw there were the Hells Angels and the Losers out of Monterrey. At that time the Losers were running as prospects to join the Angels. A couple of the Angels would bring them down because there were only three bars in Big Sur. The Angels brought prospects down to the bars in Big Sur and got them all wasted. Each prospect was to start a fight alone to begin with, but the Angels and my biker buddies and I would roll with them. They'd pick one bar one night and back everyone down, then the next night they'd pick another bar and do the same thing. It was a wild, wild, time. A free-for-all.

It's a strange process. And rough. A guy looked for any excuse to start a fight and then jumped somebody. Then the whole group ganged up on him. Of course, the other people in the bar stepped in to help. Sometimes the vacationing people were too intimidated, but local people stepped in to help. We had good fights and sometimes people would draw. Not guns, but beer bottles, chairs, flask handles, and pool cue sticks. I rarely saw guns or knives. Most of the time, we locals held our own.

A couple of times, the gangers grabbed one or two guys and really walloped them. I tried to stop it, but the owner made me a bartender and said I couldn't step out from behind the bar. It was a law. I remember one time this guy rammed another guy's face into the corner of a window. I went over there and helped the guy out of the window. I grabbed him, pulled him back behind the bar, and took him into the kitchen. I couldn't get to the hostile guy because there were 30 Hells Angels in between him and me. That's why I got the hurt dude back there. I'm surprised they didn't jump me, but they wouldn't hit a bartender back then. It was crazy. There was no law down in Big Sur. Once, the manager called the sheriff. A few days later a deputy showed up, but he got all over the manager and said, "If you guys can't control your bar we're going to have to pull your license."

He acted like it was a big inconvenience for us to call the sheriff's department. I told him we could handle it and said, "Well, you ain't going to do anything to control the crowd, so I guess we'll have to."

Later that night when Hell's Angels were there, the bar manager went into the store room and locked the door behind him. The president of the motorcycle club kicked the door in and went in and grabbed the manager. He pulled him out, threw him out in the room, and said, "No police, no phone calls." Somebody called the sheriff's department anyway, but no deputies came down for a couple of days. They wanted no business in the fight. Plus, they were miles away in Monterrey.

We had a big time rumble one night. Five Hells Angels showed up with about 25 Losers who were running prospect. That night it was our bar. They got in there, and right away they went to the pool hall. They were all doped up. I spotted one of the old timers and immediately knew what was going on: heart check. They wanted to see how those prospects would handle themselves in a bar room fight. The Angels jumped two guys who were totally pacifists. They were beating the snot out of them, so I flipped and ran out to fight this one guy, Mueller. He was six inches taller than I was and had a good 100 pounds on me. He had hold of one of his victims and was rubbing the guy's face into the corner of a shelf. He was grinding his face into the wood. Even when I ran out there, Mueller wouldn't let the man go, so I grabbed a rifle. I stuck the rifle under Mueller's nose. I said, "Back off or I'm going to blow your head off." He just kind of looked at me, but he did let go of the guy.

I dragged the bloody dude into the kitchen and then I turned around to go fight. My boss was there, and he said, "You can't. You're not even allowed to come out from behind the bar. California law. Bartender cannot step out from behind the bar."

I said, "That's true, but if anybody crosses over to my side of the bar, I'm God, and I can shoot him dead because as far as I know he's going to rob the place, right?

The Angels and Losers knew that law. None of them came over to the bar. Then I yelled, "The bar is closed. Get out of here!"

The head of the Angels said, "I'm buying the whole bar a round."

I said, "No, you're not. I'm not selling you nothing."

My boss was sitting there going, "Bob, sell them the drinks, sell them the drinks."

I said, "No, I'm not selling them nothing." The Angel got ticked off at me, but he knew I was holding a .357 on my side of the bar.

He just smiled at me. He said, "I know the law."

Then my boss pressured me into selling them a drink and asked, "One for you?"

I said, "No, I don't want a drink from you." The bikers took the drinks and then they left. A month later, they went and hit Nepenthe's and started a big brawl up there. Nepenthe's is a restaurant on the coast on Highway 1. The other bar around was the River Inn, and it was up the road north of us. Nepenthe's was south of us. We got word they were coming again, so all of the top guys in Big Sur met at our bar. When the Angels came in that time, we were ready. We were ready to rumble. I got some guys to hustle a few dice games. They were, on purpose, belligerent toward the Angels. We were trying to start a fight because we wanted to battle them this time. We had as many guys as they did, and we figured we'd whoop their butts, but they were smart enough not to stir up anything at all. They left. That was that.

The people in Big Sur learned to take care of their business *themselves*. It was reminiscent of the Old West. Some crazy stuff went on down there.

I don't know if I should talk about this or not, but I remember one time we formed a vigilante committee because some of the hippies that were in the area jumped an old man. They were camping on his property and had a campfire he thought might get out of control. He told them to clear out. He was an old man, like 70 years old, and they beat him to a pulp. All the locals then had a meeting, and we decided to form a vigilante committee. We knew where this crowd was living up in the mountains. We raided them one night. We took big buckets filled with sheep dip, and we carried wooden bristle brushes. We jumped those hippies, stripped them down to nothing, and doused them in the sheep dip. We clubbed them with the wooden brushes and told them, "Think twice before you attack a local again, especially an old man."

Then we went back to work thinking it was all over with. A few days later these two suits walked into the lodge. They showed badges and said they were FBI. They said, "We want to talk to you."

I said, "All right. Go ahead and talk. What's on your mind?"

They said, "Well, that camp you guys and your vigilantes raided the other night . . . we're not happy about that."

I said, "I don't know what you're talking about."

They said, "Well, there were two undercover agents in with them, and we didn't appreciate them being stripped down and thrown into sheep dip and spanked with wooden bristle brushes."

I was trying really hard not to laugh because the agents were so serious. It struck me as funny. I said, "Well, I know nothing about that."

They said, "Yes, well, we're telling you right now, don't let it happen again."

I just laughed it off and told many other people down in Big Sur. They got a kick out of it, too. We didn't know they were undercover agents. All we knew was that an old timer had been beaten up really badly, and we were trying to make that right.

One night some guys broke into my house while I was out on a date. I unlocked my cabin and as soon as I opened the door, I saw a guy standing there with my pistol. He said, "If you try to throw us out of your house I'm gonna splatter your brains against the wall."

I just put my hands in the air, backed up real slow, then turned and said, "Hey, the house is yours." I walked across the road to my coworker Johnny's place. He had borrowed one of my rifles. I said, "Hey, Johnny, I need my rifle and all the ammunition you've got for it."

He said, "What's up?"

I said, "I have got some crazies in my house. They're getting into my guns. I'm going to have to roust them out of there." He handed me my rifle and some shells, and he grabbed one of his pistols. Johnny and I hid down behind a huge tree that had recently fallen in the yard. We shot into the house. The guys fired back, and we started exchanging shots at each other. All the neighbors heard us.

I knew the bullets wouldn't go through that tree, and I was mostly firing over the roof just trying to scare them out of the house. The lodge

52

manager came down. He was a good friend of mine. He said somebody had called the sheriff's department. Well, this time they actually showed up. They walked up to the door and banged on it until the guys opened the door. The deputies pulled the crazies outside.

One guy had a really long beard. The lodge manager grabbed the guy by the beard and held his fist up. He had his fist cocked by the side of the guy as he pulled the guy by his beard to the end of the porch. Then he punched him with his fist. It was one of the funniest things I've ever seen. I was lying behind that log just laughing my butt off. The cops got the crazies out of the house and arrested them for using profane language in front of women and children. They got a couple of days in jail and a fine.

Big Sur was a crazy time in my life. People would come into the community and just shoplift, break into businesses, or stir up trouble. One time, this guy was in a bar, and he stole $20 right off the cocktail waitress's tray. Her husband worked in the lodge, too. He said to me, "See that big guy sitting down there in the corner?"

I said, "Yeah. He's a lot bigger than me and taller, too."

He said, "Well, he ripped twenty dollars off Pam. He's going to use the pay phone now."

So, we followed him outside. We walked up to him and asked him if the pay phone was working. Right as he answered, I kicked him in the crotch. My kick lifted him about a foot in the air, and I jumped up and hit him with everything I had. I told him, "Let's call it a draw," but the guy rolled and came up with his fists. I thought, *Oh, no. You're in trouble now.* The dude started talking right away, but I hit him again and said, "Now, let that be a lesson to you. You don't steal money from a cocktail waitress. I want that twenty dollars back." We wanted him to apologize to Pam, but he just gave us the money and took off.

One time I was bouncing at the bar door and had to check IDs when people came in; these guys from up north showed up. I asked, "You got your IDs?"

One of the men pulled a knife out, held it to my belly, and said, "Here's my ID."

I had a sawed-off shotgun right beside me. I didn't fire, but I used it as a club. He whined and begged, "Stop, stop, stop." He left and walked down the road, saying, "I'm not afraid of nobody with a gun."

Tempers were flaring in Big Sur in those days. I got in fights with Bohemians and wanderers, hippies and outlaws, thieves; you name it.

We had deep, wide stairs going up into the restaurant from the bottom of the lodge. One time, these guys came in and threw their sleeping bags out, covering the stairs and lying down on them. As women walked by, the men looked up their dresses and said nasty stuff to them.

The lady who ran the store came over and got me and said, "You've got to get rid of those men."

I walked over and asked them, "That's all your gear?"

They said, "Yes."

I said, "Pack it up and hit the road."

One dude got mouthy with me, and I just cold-cocked him. I knocked him completely out. His pals picked him up, got all their stuff, and started down the road. When they got a few dozen yards away, they yelled back at me and flipped me off. Then they made a big, big mistake.

They started building a campfire right underneath a *No Trespassing* sign. They didn't know I was the caretaker of that property, too. It belonged to an elderly woman who lived on the other side of the street. I watched over it for her. By that time, I'd bought a motorcycle. I rode my chopper down there where those guys were camped out. I put the kickstand down, shut off my bike, and jumped off. My coworker Johnny was a little Italian guy. He liked to fight. He got on his bike and rode in that direction behind me.

I said to the guys, "All right, who's got the big mouth?"

One of them smarted off, "What are you going to do about it?"

I nailed him. I hit him and it was beautiful. He was about three feet high off the ground and hit a redwood tree. He was out.

Johnny got all mad and yelled, "Bob, wait for me!"

He finally got his bike down to where I was and grabbed the other guy. He sat on top of him and popped him. Bam! Bam! Bam! Unfortunately, Johnny missed once and hit the pavement so hard he broke his wrist. Anyway, we got our point across and told them to hit the road.

Johnny went to the emergency room and got his wrist set and a cast put on. While he did that, I went back to work for about four hours. Later, this car pulled up. Two mummies sat in the back seat. They had the wire things holding their arms, wore nose plates, and were covered head to toe in bandages. A big guy got out of the car. He walked right up to me and said, "You the guy that whooped on my sons?"

I said, "Well, that depends who your sons are."

He said, "Right there."

I said, "They look familiar."

He said, "Why'd you whoop them?"

I told him what they had done in the lodge and about the derogatory remarks they had made to the women. He thought about it and said, "You know, I came up here to whoop your butt. You know what, though? They deserved what they got. They really deserved what they got." He went back and got in the car, and I could hear him yelling at them as he drove away.

The lifestyle in Big Sur was violent. I was in a fight a day, every day, and sometimes two or three fights in a day. The area is beautiful, but it was anything but peaceful. It was shady. Since then, I've never had a period in my life where I fought as much as I did there, even in prison.

Everything was drug-related. There were all kinds of drugs around: LSD, marijuana, hashish, opium, heroin, pills, and a lot of alcohol. Yes, and everybody there, even old guys, were on drugs.

It was a strange place with only a few bars, a half dozen restaurants, some hotels and campgrounds, and stores, but millions and millions of people visited in the summertime. There are tiny settlements like where I lived, but most people did day trips. The traffic on Route 1 could back up for miles. Back then, ironically, if you think about the fighting, the vibe was definitely Bohemian. People camped legally and illegally. Some say Big Sur was a pressure cooker for the hippie movement, thanks to Esalen Institute.

Esalen Institute is a retreat complex on the cliffs above the Pacific Ocean where people do self-improvement stuff. They have mineral hot tubs. Back then (maybe now), people got naked and got in the same tub. Supposedly, the mineral water cures all kinds of ills. You go there to work on your inner-self. It never made sense to me. Joan Baez taught classes there. Nancy Carlen and some other folk singers, including Joan Baez, kicked off a yearly festival at Esalen. In 1969, there were so many people that we had shuttle buses running 40 miles between the lodge and the Institute. Big Sur is almost dead center between San Francisco and Los Angeles, and just below Monterey. If you read about the Esalen Institute, you'll find a lot of history, especially to do with hippies, Jack Kerouac, LSD, and out-of-body experiences.

I started playing bongos when I was about twelve, but I graduated to the conga drum. Mom bought me my first set and I've been playing all my life. By the time I was seventeen, I was a solid conga drummer. When I split to California, which, of course, was in the in the '60s, I played with some cool people. Just after the roads opened up from the mudslides, there was a wedding in the meadow near the campground in our settlement. This woman lived there in that meadow, and she was connected with everybody. She knew actors, actresses, and producers and knew one of the owners of the lodge. She was helping the people hosting the wedding, and Santana was going to play the music. Well, Carlos, another guitar player, a bass player, and a keyboard player showed up, but the percussion section drove right by and missed the location. They somehow wound up in Los Angeles.

I was sitting there in front of the camp store playing my drums. A guy walked up and asked, "Hey you. Do you want to play with us?"

I didn't know him, but I said, "Sure." We played for six hours, and when we finished, my joints were bleeding. When we shut it down, my buddy Saul came up to me and said, "Do you know who that was?"

I said, "Yeah, Carlos."

He said, "Dude, you don't know who Carlos Santana is? He is a recording star."

I said, "I've never heard of him." The band was just cutting an album and their first hit song was "Evil Ways," if I remember right. Maybe it was "Black Magic Woman." Santana is still playing today—with Rob Thompson, I think. Carlos was an excellent guitar player. Anyway, they had a young lady singing with them. I can't remember her name. What a beautiful voice she had. I partied with them.

Some guys and I started a group. Danny, our lead guitar player, had an opportunity to play with Loretta Lynn. The only thing that stopped him was that her managers said he'd have to join the union. He was totally anti-union, so he turned them down. We did cut an album. Well, I had a connection with Circle Records that handled most of the West Coast. I told her about our group. She said, "Give me some albums and I'll put them into stores and sell them."

I talked to Danny about it, and he said, "No. We're just going to keep the albums [all 10,000 of them], and we'll sell them at our concerts."

I said, "Danny, nobody makes it like that." He didn't care if we got paid.

Not long after that, he met the girl of his dreams. This guy had talent. He could play any instrument there is, but he had *mastered* 28 of them. He could compose, create music, write lyrics; you name it. And, he was in love. One night, he and his girl did their thing. He woke up in the morning and reached over to her, but she was cold. She died in her sleep. After that he started drinking hard. He got an infection in his right arm and doctors wound up amputating it. That was the end of his music career. It's a shame. Danny Phillips was the man. He wrote over 500 songs. He reminded me of Marshall Tucker, Charlie Daniels, and the Eagles. We played a lot of their stuff, along with the music Danny wrote.

My all-time favorite rock and roll song is Marshal Tucker's "24 Hours at a Time." I love the version when they invited Charlie Daniels up on stage to play the fiddle.

Many other groups came down there. Big Sur was the hang out. Studios filmed many movies around the area. I used to go up to Carmel-by-the-Sea and the other direction down to Lake Arrowhead all the time on my motorcycle. Carmel is beautiful. That's where Clint Eastwood was the mayor. We had a naval base just north of us. It was a top-secret submarine tracking station. They used sound surveillance systems, which were underwater posts around the world, to track Soviet subs during the Cold War. We hired a lot of the Navy guys to come in and tend bar and do other jobs. I had a really good friend who worked up at the tracking base. One day he was drunk, so I asked him, "What do you do down there?" He was instantly sober.

He said, "I can't tell you that, Bob. You know I have to report that you even asked me."

I said, "Well, go ahead. It doesn't bother me. I was just curious about what you're doing."

STARS

I MET SEVERAL MOVIE STARS. We had one or two who lived there in Big Sur while the rest had vacation properties there or stayed nearby. Some of them did drugs, some of them were big drinkers, but most were nice. There was only one I didn't get along with very well, and I'd rather not mention her name because if it comes out in the book, people may take offense. She's the type of person who would file a lawsuit. Her personality was rough unless you dropped down on your knees and worshipped her. Even when she was at the height of her career, she never said or did anything pleasant toward me. I mean, I treated her with respect, but when she flashed her eyelashes at me and talked in her low, deep voice, she did absolutely nothing for me. One night I was jamming at the bar, and she yelled at me to wait on her and said something like, "Don't you know who I am?"

I just walked up to her and said, "I don't care who you are. Do you want a drink or not?" I never thought she was that hot, and I guess that's why we were enemies because she expected me to drop to my knees and say, "Oh, famous actress, can I have your autograph?" She was just another customer, and because I had that attitude, we didn't get along. She and I took an instant dislike to each other.

When I was out working at the gas station, she'd whine, "Don't forget my local discount." In '69-'70, fuel was 69 cents a gallon down there, and locals got ten cents off per gallon. She was always complaining about me, but the owners knew how she was. They didn't like her either. It just went in one ear and out the other. From what I knew of her, she was real nasty to other people, too.

Property in Big Sur was very expensive. Back then it went for $11,000 an acre. Stars and rich people had second homes up in the redwood trees. A limited amount of land was available because the government protected most of it. They still do. Mike Kellin was around. He did a movie called *The Wackiest Ship in the Army*. He played a chief mate, I think. I got to meet him. He was down to earth.

Like I said, Clint Eastwood was there, up in Carmel. One time, Clint Eastwood was actually staying in the lodge motel in Big Sur. All these little old ladies got outside his room at about six in the morning. I was opening up the gas station and heard the women calling him, "Clint, Clint, come out. Come out, Clint, we want to see you." Well he did. He walked out of the motel room door and yawned really big. The ladies all screamed and covered their eyes because he was stark naked. I got the biggest kick out of it because they were hiding their eyes with their fingers *open*.

I met the guy who played Illya Kuryakin on *The Man from U.N.C.L.E.* He plays Ducky now on *NCIS*. His name is David McCallum. A buddy of mine ran a nearby campground and he called me up. I was at the bar. He said, "Bob, I got a family here, husband and wife and two little kids, and they want to camp someplace, but they don't want to camp in a campground where there are a lot of people. They want to camp someplace secluded." He knew I had a campsite in the back of my house, and he said, "Would you care if they camped in your backyard?"

I said, "No problem. I'll leave the back door open, too. Tell them they're more than welcome to come in and use the restroom and kitchen."

My house was on the Redwood Lodge property. It came with the job and was nice. The house had a big living room and kitchen area, a big bathroom, and then there was a ladder that went up to the loft. I slept in the loft. The heat in the winter came from a good wood stove.

So David McCallum and his wife and kids camped in the backyard. One night after I got off work from closing the bar, I heard light knocking on my back door. I answered the door, and a little boy looked up and said, "My mom and dad would like to invite you over for a glass of wine." I said I'd be right over. I recognized the man but didn't say anything. I just sat there. We drank some wine, played some chess, and I smoked a joint or two.

When I was leaving he said, "I guess you didn't recognize me."

I said, "No, I know who you are, but I figured you wanted to be secluded, so you're probably tired of people hounding you for autographs and everything else."

He said, "Yes. I can't go anywhere without getting mobbed by people." I guess privacy was important. He stayed in my backyard for a week.

Then I met the little boy who played Timmy on the original *Lassie* series. Jon Provost was his name. He was all grown. Many dogs played Lassie, and he had one of the dogs that was Lassie. I said, "You must be well off now from that series. You guys played on TV for many years."

He said, "No, my parents made most of the money. After a while, I left Hollywood and moved to Northern California."

I met a lot of other actors and actresses, and most of them were fairly good people. I met Henry Miller. Actually, I used to play chess with Henry Miller down at Nepenthe. It's a famous world-class restaurant, and there's also a boutique gift shop, a stone fireplace, and an awesome patio about 1,000 feet above the coast.

Hollywood made quite a few movies with scenes at Nepenthe. One popular movie filmed there is *The Sandpi*per with Richard Burton and Elizabeth Taylor. I didn't meet them, but I met so many other movie people. I lived with one actress for a while. Her name was Adrian, and she was an actress in a Canadian movie studio. The only movie that I saw her in was filmed in Canada. Her character and another guy robbed a bank. At the end they're trying to get away on a motorcycle. They go to jump off the road, and they wind up going through a barbed wire fence. They did their own stunts. She had a strip of skin ripped out of her arm. She was very self-conscious about it.

Big Sur was a wild place, not just because of the people, but also because of the animals. While I lived there, I went wild boar hunting. I met this young lady named Diana Burroughs. She was the granddaughter to Edgar Rice Burroughs. He owned a big estate in southern Big Sur. Diana got me a permit so I could hunt on his estate for wild boar. Now old man William Randolph Hearst, the guy that owned the newspapers, brought over Russian wild boar and crossbred them with American pigs on his ranch. They ended up loose all over

California. They're huge. The record boar was over in King City. From the back of the head (the back of the ears) to the end of the two curls of the horns was four feet. There's a new record now of a 733-pound boar killed by a guy from Oakdale on a private ranch near Fort Bragg. That's the record, but I've seen them bigger than that. I've seen them when they stood in front of my pickup truck and blocked both headlights at the same time. They were as big as cows. You don't hunt them. Their meat is too tough to eat. You want to get the young ones that weigh under 200 pounds.

I used to take people up there hunting at eight dollars apiece and guarantee them a pig. Two days before I was going up there to hunt, I'd go around to the local restaurants and collect all their food garbage, mostly the vegetables. I'd go up and spread the food out on the side of the hill, and then we'd come up a couple of days later. The pigs were usually in there rooting and eating the food. I always told hunters, "You want to get the young pigs unless you're hunting for a trophy. If you want the meat, go no bigger than 200 pounds." They got their pigs and paid me $100.

I loved doing that, but one night I was up there checking on things and actually got spooked. I was taking a party out the next day. It was late night and a full moon was shining. As I crawled up a steep trail on the hill, I heard a mountain lion growling on my left side. On the right, I heard a wolf growling. They came closer and closer. Suddenly, they jumped each other right on top of my back. I let out a yell you would not believe. The lion went left. The wolf ran right. I took off straight back down the hill. I ran all the way.

There were lots of mountain lions up there. I remember one time a friend and I were on the Burroughs estate, and we had some new dogs we were going to try out. This hunter friend of mine had just bought the dogs. They were expensive, about a hundred bucks apiece. We hiked up to the top of the hill and signaled to some other guys with a flashlight. Those guys released the dogs, and the dogs drove the pigs up to us, where we could pick them off. I went one way, and my buddy went the other to get set up. I stopped to go to the bathroom, and, just as I started going, I looked up into the trees and saw a mountain lion perched on branch and looking down at me. I wet all over my pants. I couldn't have done anything to defend myself. The lion was licking his lips, probably tasting my scent and making his plan of attack. I managed to slowly walk away, but I was shaking so hard that my friend automatically knew. He said, "You ran into old Snagglepuss." The locals knew the lion. He said the animal had never attacked, but I wasn't convinced. Really, the only time mountain lions attack people is when they're too old to hunt fast animal prey. I guess people are slow . . . easier to get.

DRUGS

I WASN'T PARTYING WITH DRUGS MUCH. When I first got to California, I'd already given up heroin, so in general, I cooled it for a while. I met a girl named Cheryl from Tennessee and was in love. We got engaged, but then she broke my heart. Cheryl was the granddaughter of the woman who ran the camp store. She went to college in Tennessee but came to Big Sur to work for the summer. We started going out and we clicked. I fell in love hard. I asked her to marry me, and she said, "Yes."

Several weeks later, on my birthday, we went to see *Butch Cassidy and the Sundance Kid*. I drove Cheryl back to her grandmother's house and parked the car. She took the ring off and handed it back to me and said plainly, "Happy birthday."

I looked at her ring in my hand and said, "What's this?"

She said, "You didn't think I was serious, did you?"

I said, "Well, yes. I thought you were."

She said, "Oh, no. This is just a summer fling."

It broke my heart. I was about 23 years old.

She led me on big time. She broke up with me because she was leaving to go back to school in a couple of weeks. The day she was leaving she came to see me and wanted to kiss me. I wouldn't kiss her. I said, "What's the point?"

I didn't date for about two years at all. I didn't even dance unless a girl was a good friend of mine and asked me. Otherwise, I said, "No, thank you."

Life changed after that. Big Sur was wild and an easy place to be wild. The drug culture was strong, and I became a big part of it. I sold pot as a side job. I was actually making more money dealing pot than I was working my regular jobs. I got good money for a kilo. At that time, marijuana sold for about fifteen dollars per ounce. I didn't grow it. I had connections. Those people brought me the pot. I bought from them, sold it to other people, and kept the profits. At one point, I had several people working for me. I never sold to anyone I didn't know. Even if some guy came up to me and offered a thousand dollars for a joint, I'd say, "I don't know what you are talking about." He might be a narc. I think pot should be legal. Now that I'm sick, my doctor prescribed it so I might have more of an appetite and less pain. I did it for a while, but since I got out of the hospital I haven't touched it. I just don't like doing it now. I hate the way it makes me feel. I don't like being high anymore, which is funny because I used to pay good money to feel that way.

CONTACT

I WAS LONELY. I had no ties, no reason to stay anywhere, really. I definitely had no family on that side of the country. I did drag my brother Donnie and my friend Saul, who I considered a brother because we'd been partners in all kinds of stuff for years, out to California. I heard that Donnie was bad on drugs back home, and I knew Saul was into heroin. When they came to California, I told both of them, "Look here. I'm not going to let you do any more heroin." I put the word out on the street to steer clear of Donnie and Saul and threatened that if anybody so much as gave them the cotton they used to filter the stuff I'd pounce. I was a violent guy, so most people didn't give them any. Unfortunately, one guy did.

I came home from work and my brother was passed out on my bed. He was as high as a kite and had puked in the sheets. I grabbed him hard. He picked up a bottle of wine and tried to hit me with it. I blocked it and I hit him, broke his nose, and he fell down. I said, "Where did you get the heroin?" He wouldn't tell me but I found out, and I went down and paid a visit to that guy. I said, "You knew what I said. I told you personally not to give drugs to my brother. You did wrong, man. He needs to be sober."

He said, "Donnie's a grown man. What are you going to do about it?"

I broke both of his elbows. I grabbed both of his arms and twisted him around. I held him with one hand and picked up a baseball bat with the other. I came down as hard as I could. I snapped one, then the other. I said, "Now go shoot yourself up."

He wound up leaving Big Sur. He knew that if he stuck around there, every time I saw him I'd beat him up. Donnie split, too. I think he moved up to San Francisco. I lost contact with him in 1970. I never saw him again. Saul moved up to Oregon and worked at a lumber camp. One time I drove up to Eugene to look for him, but he wasn't there. By the time I drove that way, he had moved on and was working on a fishing boat catching Alaskan king crab. I lost contact with him, too.

66

KINGMAN

I STAYED IN BIG SUR A LITTLE OVER THREE YEARS. I liked the new manager who came in and took over the lodge. We got to be really good friends. He and his wife owned some land over in Kingman, Arizona, and decided to move there. They invited me to come along, and I said, "Well, sure. I've never been in the desert." I moved to Kingman Easter Sunday of 1971. All the big moves of my life have happened on Easter Sunday.

Back then, Kingman was a funky drunk western town. Kingman, at that time, was really small with fewer than 3,000 people living there. Now there are 40,000 or 50,000 people in the area. I got a job right away as soon as I got there. I waited tables at Denny's and helped out as a prep cook. For a while I slept in a tent behind my friend's house, but when summer came around it was too hot. I rented a little apartment downtown. I had sold my motorcycle and didn't have a car, so I had to walk about two miles to work, but I didn't mind. I worked the night shift, so the walk to work in the evening was cool and even cooler in the morning on my way home at about six. I had a swamp cooler, and I slept right under it. That thing went full blast. The apartment building was right by the train tracks, and all day long trains rolled by and shook the whole apartment. My rent was about $25 a week.

I switched jobs and made good money as a mechanic. I was good at saving, too. I wanted to live in the desert, so I looked for a place out there. The real estate agent talked me into buying a five-bedroom house with acreage, all fenced in and out in the middle of nowhere in Golden Valley. It was high desert. I had 40 acres and it was mostly sand, but there were a lot of small little mesquite bushes, a lot of juniper here and there, a lot of cactus, and tons and tons of rattlesnakes. The hardest thing about living in the desert was the long, inconvenient ride into town. I worked in town, but that was about it. I remember driving home at night through Golden Valley, which was about, I don't know, maybe ten to fifteen miles across. There were only two lights that you could see out there in Golden Valley. One was a pizza parlor and then on the other side of the road, about two miles down from that, was another light. That light came from my house. Those were the only lights visible there. Now if you go out across there, it's lit up like a city with wall-to-wall houses. As much as I could, I stayed out in the wild on my ranch because I had a lot to take care of there when I wasn't at work in town.

To earn extra money, my buddy Norris Anderson started a side business. We looked for old abandoned barns all the time. We peeled the boards off and took them home to make coffee tables to sell. We built the legs out of two-by-four cross braces and used the old barnwood planks as tops. We sanded the wood smooth as glass, then we scraped out sections, chipped little holes, and used pencil soldering guns to burn intricate designs like native birds and peacocks. In the chipped areas, we embedded turquoise and Apache teardrops into the wood. Apache teardrop is a shiny black stone that looks like a black pearl. We also found and used fire agate and fire opal. Anywhere there was a copper mine, we found several stones that we would lay into the tables. We also painted on them with oil-based enamels. We sealed the tables with five coats of Varathane to make the surfaces nice and smooth. Norris and I got $500 apiece for those tables. We couldn't make them fast enough for the doctors. All of the doctors wanted "Tables by Bob and Norris."

Life on the ranch was peaceful. The wildlife was incredible. One day, I was out working on the fence line. I happened to look across at another fence line, and I saw these two huge dogs. One was white and one was gray. They looked like big afghans with long fur. I watch them run across the desert and I thought, *Somebody lost his dogs.* I mentioned it to an old cowboy buddy of mine. He said, "Those weren't dogs."

I said, "What were they then?"

He said, "Those are desert wolves. You're lucky you saw them. They are very, very rare."

Yes, I saw so much wildlife out there: coyotes, wolves, mountain lions, bighorn sheep. At the far end of Golden Valley, there was a road that went down to Nevada, and there were mountains right there. If I drove there in the mornings, I saw bighorn sheep on the sides of mountains. It's cool to see them. Some people hunt them, but the country's so rugged, you have to be a mountaineer to get in there to shoot one, and then it's going to be a real bear to get the sheep out of there. If I went into the mountains and the foothills, I also found mule deer. They're not like New England deer.

I hunted on the ranch quite a bit. One thing I really liked to hunt was quail. Golden Valley was just loaded with quail. I could go down into a wash and just sit and wait. Quail are delicious. They're rich in flavor. They kind of remind me a Cornish game hen because they're about that size. I hunted dove and water ducks. There were a lot of wild mallards. I hunted cottontail rabbits, too. That was a lot of fun.

ANIMALS

I RAISED LOTS OF ANIMALS. On the ranch I had pigs, cows, horses, goats, cats, dogs, and chickens. I shot jackrabbits and cut them up to feed to the chickens. Chickens are like cannibals, you know. I had this one old billy goat who was a royal pain. He'd look at me and jump the fence. That is no joke. I had four strands of barbed wire, so the top strand was about up to my chest. The goat would walk over to the fence, stare me right in the eyes, and jump straight up and over the wire. Then off he'd go into the desert. Time after time I had to track him down. Sometimes it took a couple days to catch him. Once I did, I put a rope around him, but he always refused to follow me. He locked his legs and held his ground. Most of the time I just picked him up, put him on my back, and carried him. As soon as I did that, he peed down my back. Every time. I got tired of it. One day, he pulled his tricks again. I had just brought him back from the desert. He looked over at me, and I looked at him like, "Don't do it." He jumped right over the fence. So, I grabbed my rifle. I always kept my rifle with me. I shot him in the head. I cooked him up and had him for dinner. I wasn't chasing after him again. You could say we weren't that close. I don't even know if he had a name. I think I called him *Nitwit* or something like that. He was an escape artist. He was a character.

I had other animals that were cool, like range ponies. My cows were white-faced Herefords. Because Kingman is desert, I was only allowed to have X number of cows with my bull. The government comes in and tells you how many cows you can have on your land because there are no trees unless you plant them and irrigate the soil. I bought bales of hay, the three band bales. They were 90 pounds each and cost only a dollar and a quarter a bale. Now, two band bales, which are only about 70 pounds, are about seven or eight bucks. Feed has gone way, way up. When the feed goes up, the price of meat goes up. I always tried to grow my own meat, and the chickens supplied me with eggs, and when they weren't laying, they were dinner. I went and had a talk with them in the mornings. I'd say, "Okay, here's the deal. You can provide breakfast or

70

you can be dinner." When they were mating with the rooster, I'd always hatch them up so the hens could sit on their eggs. It took only 21 days, and then I'd get a new crop of them going. If you start off with four or five hens and a rooster you are well on your way and don't have to buy anymore unless a fox or something gets in there and kills them all off. I usually kept about twenty chickens, total.

The first spring alone I killed fourteen rattlesnakes. That's why I always kept a rifle with me. I shot most of them, but one day I opened the back door and a rattler was right there on the ground. He struck at me. I hit him with the door. He tried to get in, so I grabbed my pistol off the nearby counter and shot him. Another time, I was doing something in the garage, and I heard this buzzing sound. I looked toward the sound and saw a fat rattlesnake about four or five feet away from me. He was curled up and just buzzing his rattle away, getting ready to strike. I ran into the house, grabbed my gun, came out, and started shooting at him. I missed and hit the concrete floor. The bullet ricocheted and stunned the snake. Then he took off under my freezer. I ran over and tilted the freezer up. I shot him and hit him three times, but one bullet when through the refrigeration line. The stuff coming out of the line partially froze him. He was *still* trying to get away, so I dropped the freezer down on top of him. That chopped him in half.

I collected the rattles and had a whole can full, along with a bunch of skins. If snakes I killed were big enough, I cleaned and cooked them. Snake meat is tasty. I got a big pot and filled it about a third of the way up with oil. Then I mixed up a beer batter. The snake meat cut nicely into small little pieces about four to six inches long. I dipped the pieces in the batter and dropped them in the hot oil, like a deep fry. Most people like it if they don't know what they are eating.

Besides all the animals, I grew an orchard of peach trees and a huge garden. The soil out on my ranch was so rich. I could grow anything I wanted. All I had to do was put water to it. I had to drill down over a thousand feet to get the well, but it was the sweetest water I've ever had, and it was an underground ocean. The Duval copper mine company had half a dozen wells down in the area. These wells were giant. Duval used the water in their mines. I forget what they called the process, but they split water somehow and washed the oil out. There were quite a few copper mines all over Arizona. I raised an acre of corn to feed the animals I butchered (I always put them on corn for three months before I butchered them). It drove me nuts because my luck with the corn crop was bad. When it came time to harvest, I pulled the silks down and there wouldn't be a single kernel. Worms got to the whole acre some years. It was frustrating, so I wound up buying feed, mostly hay, down in Bullhead City. Back then, I could get a ton of hay for a good price as long as I hauled it myself. I had an old 1950 Dodge pickup truck with a flathead six-cylinder engine and a low railroad gearbox. I couldn't go more than 50 miles an hour downhill, but that truck could haul a lot on twin axles. That truck had to climb from almost sea level up to 3,000 feet in just four miles of road. It walked, but it made it.

DESERT

I LOVED ARIZONA WEATHER. It is hot all the time except for about three months of cooler weather. Usually, in December, you get a break for a little bit but don't get a freeze until the middle of January. I liked the 70-degree days and 40-degree nights, all in the same week. The rainy season comes in March with a steady drizzle that lasts on through to May. Then, summer hits and days are hot. The good thing is that it is so dry there that you are still comfortable most of the time even though it gets up to 100 degrees and higher. As long as you move there in the winter, you can become acclimated to the heat.

Arizona weather is awesome to study. In summer you can be enjoying a clear beautiful day and the sky suddenly turns black, telling you a sandstorm is coming. The sandstorms I saw were amazing. I loved sandstorms. They'd start at one end of the Golden Valley, and I could see them from about 40 miles away. Whenever one kicked up, I watched its black wall as it came toward me. I used to get into my truck and roll up the windows to sit and watch storms from inside them. When a sandstorm hit, it would literally cover the truck in darkness for about five minutes. The truck rocked back and forth. Then with that came huge thunderstorms and sometimes jumbo marbles of hail. They call a sandstorm-rainstorm combination a *haboob.* Storms are serious in the desert. That was one thing you always had to be careful about because heavy rains cause desert dry washes. Basically, flat areas of really dry soil can flood super-fast and become dangerous in a matter of minutes. They are like dried up riverbeds that turn into rivers. Sometimes, when you get really bad cloudbursts, the washes overflow their own banks, and they create new unpredictable washes. What happens is the rain hits miles in the distance. You might not even know it's coming your way. Then you see a little trickle of water coming down a wash. Suddenly, the water is gone and foam takes its place. The foam is about a foot high. That's your sign to get out of the way because there's a wall of water coming down the wash. Depending on the depth of the water, the wall could be anywhere from three to nine or so feet high and it's held up by a wall of brush that rolls and rolls down the wash. If you get in a wash's water, you don't have a chance to survive, especially at the very beginning because that wall of water and rolling trees and branches across the front of the wash can crush you. It doesn't take long for that heavy brush being pushed by thousands of gallons of water to knock you off your feet and you are gone. The force of the water coming down is unbelievable.

During the monsoon season, too, you get rain you could set your watch by. I remember a season when every day at three in the afternoon, we got thunderstorms. Then we got the flash floods. There were a couple of times when they hit really hard. Those washes are powerful enough to sweep a car. I remember one time this tourist family went through a main wash that stretched across the highway. I don't know what the guy was thinking, but he tried to drive across it, and it just swept him and his family down the wash. His bad decision drowned all of them—the husband, the wife, and two children. Once, a deputy sheriff tried to go through a wash. He drowned, too. It might look like the road is there, but there's a huge hole and the water is deep and fast. The water rolls the car and the windshield breaks. Later, the car is found twenty miles away buried in the mud.

My ranch was isolated, so that was scary. My road from the highway down to my house was two miles, and there were several washes that ran through that road. I was driving home from work late one night and all of a sudden, I was airborne. I nosed down into an eight-foot drop. The wash had taken the road. It was completely gone. I didn't see it because it was dark out. The wreck broke the motor mount on my truck, and the engine went through the radiator. Somehow, I didn't get hurt. I was upset with myself for not seeing that the road was gone, and I was upset with the county because they never put a sign up. I had two or three washes that ran into my property. I thought about digging big holes and diverting them and making a pond, but I never got around to that.

In Arizona, the state and the counties are liable for anything that happens on the roads. They are supposed to mark washes and other dangers. There are washes around Highway 68 (the road between Kingman and Bullhead City) where sometimes a quarter-mile section of the road will be under water for 24 hours. I called the county up after my wreck, and they came out. They helped me get my truck home and reimbursed me a little bit, like about half the cost of the radiator. I managed to get the belt off it. Then, I had to put in a new radiator and new motor mount. A guy who was grading the road up in Golden Valley had all the parts and stuff I needed, and he brought them out to the ranch to me. It only took me about a day or so to get the truck fixed because I had a garage, and it was easier to work inside the garage than it was outside. The bad thing is after it rains like that, the humidity is almost 100 percent, and coupled with the temperature of 110 to 120 degrees, it is murder. I was working on my truck and my whole body was soaked in about two minutes, clothes and everything. I had to drink a lot of water because I knew I could get dehydrated really quick.

If you live in the desert, you have to be aware of a lot of things. The winds that cause sandstorms are really heavy duty winds. They kick that sand up and when you know it's coming, when you see or hear the wind in the canyon, off in the distance with thunder and lightning, you'd better batten down the hatches. You have to make sure you've got plenty of food and water, first off, just in case you get isolated. The next thing is to make sure all of your windows are closed. If you're working outside, you get out of the wash and take all your tools with you because if you don't they'll wind up down in California or out in the Pacific Ocean.

I saw a picture not long ago of a sandstorm hitting Phoenix. A wall of sand probably 400 or 500 feet high, pure brown, went on for miles. That's how I remember it out in Golden Valley, too.

Man, I learned a lot in Arizona. I took courses with the National Rifle Association (NRA). I was studying to be an instructor at one point, so I took the desert survival course. Some of the lessons came in real handy, like, if you're trapped in the desert without water, how to get water by making a desert well. All you need is a piece of clear plastic and a cup. You scoop out a hole down in the desert until you get down to where the soil is damp. Then, you put your cup down in the bottom of it. You lay the plastic over the hole but don't let it touch the cup, and you seal the plastic up with sand all the way around it so it won't move.

You put a rock in the middle of the plastic until it is slanting down toward the center, forming a sort of funnel at the top. Then, as the sun beats down on it, condensation from the sand forms on the plastic. Pretty soon, drops of water roll down and drop into your cup. Depending on how damp the soil is, you can get two or three cups of water a day, which can keep you alive. I learned how to set certain snares and how to tell which direction I was going. I knew some of that already from my childhood. I've never had a problem with directions. I just follow the sun. In the morning, the sun is in the east. In the afternoon, the sun is in the west.

Always, whenever I went out, even in the woods, I always made sure to notice where I came from and where the sun was as I started out. For example, one time when I was hunting, I had to take a road. I made sure to remember which direction I walked on that road. Sure enough, I got disoriented out in the woods, but I knew I had to head west, and I thought I had walked about a mile and a half. I told myself, "I'm going to head west about a mile and a half, and I should hit the road." It worked. I've never been lost in the woods. There are a ton of people who get lost in the woods and they panic. People get lost, they lose their way, and they panic, and that's what kills people: the panic. That was one of the first things they taught us at NRA. Don't panic. If you feel yourself starting to panic just hunker down and think. Calm down and think about it and plan what you're going to do. For example, don't walk during the heat of the day. Find a bush or something you can lie down underneath that will protect you from the sun. You want to walk in the early morning or the evening or during the night. If you walk during the heat of the day from noon to about three or four in the afternoon, you are not going to make it very far. With the sun beating down on you, you're going to lose all the moisture in your body, all the water in your body. Dehydration is tough. You're walking, and the next second you're passed out on the ground. There are other ways to get water besides a desert well. With certain cactus plants, you can cut a little pulp out and put a little cup up against the stalk, and you'll get some water. I've done that several times. The water tastes bitter. Another way to find water is to follow the bees. Bumblebees will lead you to water. I learned how to find springs and things like that. Desert springs have sweet water. Look for animal tracks to make sure it's safe to drink. If there are tracks and no skeletons or dead bodies, then you know the water is good to drink. If you see animal tracks, not that many of them, and you find a skeleton, you don't want to touch the water. There's poison in it.

We can learn a lot from animals if we pay attention. Animals will tell you if a storm is coming. When sand is coming, animals, including the rabbits and birds, go to the ground. They have senses and get out of the way by burrowing down into their homes or hiding in the brush.

LOUISE

I DECIDED TO HELP THIS LADY OUT. Not long after I bought the ranch, I met Louise. She had six kids, and she was pregnant with her seventh. They all moved in with me. Renee was her oldest and had brain damage because Louise's ex-husband used to beat Louise and the kids. He took Renee one time and threw her into a wall. Her head went through the sheetrock and hit a nail. She was like a person with autism after that. Renee had a different dad, but the rest belonged to Louise's ex-husband. He resented Renee because Louise was pregnant when they got married and told him he was Renee's father, but he eventually found out the truth. He kidnapped Louise once before we were together, and one of the kids called the police. They got her away from him. They held him for a while, but they let him go. He was walking down the street a few days later and a couple of police officers had gotten off duty and had changed their clothes. They caught him on the street. They put him into an alleyway, and they beat him so badly they put him in the hospital. He didn't learn. When he got out of the hospital, he went to see Louise and beat the snot out of her again. I saw him a couple of times when he brought the kids' child support. Both times he came, Louise shook and got really nervous. I put my foot down and said, "You don't come by here again. If you come by here again I'm going to take you up in the back of the barn, and I'm going to give to you what Louise couldn't." I was a tough guy. He never came back.

When the family moved in with me, Renee was seventeen, Nancy was fifteen, Michael was twelve or thirteen, then came Jimmy, Tabby, and Danny. I think Danny was about eight. Louise was a waitress in town. My garage boss was good friends with the owner of the restaurant, and we stopped in there to eat all the time. They had daily specials, so I went there for lunch every day. Louise and I got to talking and became friends. She was much older than I was.

She told me she lost her house and had nowhere to go to with all the kids. I had that five-bedroom house, so I said, "Well, I think you can stay out on the ranch with me until you find a place." I just figured it was the right thing to do. They all moved in. Louise and I maybe went out a few times, but I wasn't romantically interested in her at all. I caught on that she wanted more from me, but I didn't love her, and I told her up front. I said, "Don't expect anything to go with this because I'm not interested in you that way." She just had this idea that ultimately I would love her. You can't make somebody love you.

When the baby was born, the doctor asked, "Who is the father?"

I said, "I think I am." I never thought he was mine. I was being polite.

Louise said, "No."

My friends told me the baby looked identical to some guy she had been seeing.

A year later, I woke up married to her. At that time, I rode with a bunch of bikers there in Kingman. We were on a motorcycle run and supposed to go down to Tucson and camp out and roll over to Firebird where they had the motorcycle races and things like that. Somehow we got our wires crossed. Half of us wound up going to Las Vegas instead. I woke up in a hotel room on Sunday morning. About six brothers who rode with us were just standing in the doorway of the room and holding magnums of champagne. They said, "Are you ready to celebrate?" I had been so drunk I didn't remember anything from the two days before.

The first thought in my head was great. I thought, *All right, I must have won a big jackpot because these guys are bringing champagne!* I asked them, "How much did I win?"

They looked at me and said, "You didn't win."

I said, "No kidding. How much did I win? You guys ordered champagne, so I must have won a good jackpot or something."

They said, "Don't you remember Friday night?"

I asked, "What day is today?"

They said, "This is Sunday."

I said, "No. I don't remember Friday or Saturday. The only memories I have are of right now. What did I do?"

They said, "You got married."

I said, "What? To who?"

"To Louise!" they yelled.

She was under the covers the whole time and sat up real fast. She said, "What do you mean 'to who?' You married me!"

Then I said, "Why? I mean, I don't love you. Have I ever told you I love you?"

She said, "No, but you will."

I said, "No, I won't because it's not there, and you can't make somebody love you if it's not there."

It was almost enough to make me quit drinking.

I had a Shovelhead Harley that I didn't get to ride all that much after that because I was with the kids. I wound up having to sell my bike. I was like their dad for a while. I got along better with the kids than I did with Louise. I took the older boys quail hunting in the mornings. We hunted in the washes. We would find a good place to stand and look around for signs like berry bushes, nut bushes, and mesquite bushes about twenty yards away. We sat with our shotguns and waited. We quietly listened to hear the quail come closer, and once the birds started showing up, we waited until six or more were in range of a shotgun. Then one of us shot. It was nothing to hit most of them using a quick blast of birdshot. My stepsons and their friends and I camped out just above the washes for a few days. We hunted lunch and dinner and cooked the birds on our little campfires. The last day, we tagged our limits and brought the quail home.

I think I was a good stepfather to them. Once, one of them did something wrong, and I spanked him. He went to school and told I spanked him. Luckily the guidance counselor said, "Well, what did *you* do?" He told the truth (I don't even remember what he did wrong), and the guidance counselor said, "No wonder your stepdad spanked you. I don't blame him."

In the '80s and '90s teachers asked kids weird stuff like, "Do your dad and mom smoke funny tobacco?" and, "Do your dad and mom put powder on their noses?" Some people went overboard and broke up families. They broke up child-parent relationships. Then again, I guess if you see a parent doing something like that, you should turn him in. My oldest stepson wanted to do the NRA classes, so I said, "Well, I'll do it with you." That's how I got started with NRA. The kids liked ranch life, and I liked having them there, but Louise and I were not a match. I thought it was going to turn out all right, but after a while I couldn't stand her, and she couldn't stand me. If I was in the room watching TV and she walked in, I got up and left. The same thing happened if I walked in a room and she was there. She got up and left. Really, it's either there or it's not there. I was right up front when I told her from the start that it wasn't going to work. Then she tricked me. Then I stuck it out for five years, but after about a year and a half it was real bad. We had separate bedrooms at either end of the house. She entered one door, and I used the other one. It got to where we could not handle the sight of each other. It then got to the point one day when the kids would choose sides, and I didn't want that. I told them. I said, "Hey, hey, wait a minute. That's your mom. You stand by your mom. Right or wrong, you stand by your mother. I'm just your stepdad, and you don't drop your mom for somebody else. Your mom is your flesh and blood. You've got to stand by her."

I left. I took my truck and drove away from the ranch. I camped out in the mountains for about two weeks and thought about everything. I realized I was starting to create more harm than I was good. It was time to leave, so I went home, grabbed most of my stuff and just told her I was leaving. I didn't want to mess the kids up. I only count Louise and me as half a marriage because I didn't deliberately marry her.

At the exact same time, I was being ripped off by the lady who sold the ranch to me. I worked hard and was a good saver. When I bought from her, I had ten acres all paid off and gave that to her like a down payment. Then, I made installments on the ranch. The lady took me really good. I paid $48,000 for 40 acres, a five-bedroom house, a barn, outbuildings, acreage all fenced in, the orchard, and a well. My payments were $225 a month, but the interest was $300 a month. At the end of almost two years I owed more money than I did to begin with. I found out that the lady who tricked me on that had an opportunity to lease the well out with a water company. Somebody was starting a water company there, and my well was down a thousand feet. I would have made $10,000 for leasing the well, but she wouldn't let me do that. I could have paid off the house with those earnings, and she wouldn't let me do it. The property was owner-financed. The old owner said, "You now owe $60,000."

I said, "Wait a minute. How do I owe you more? I gave you 10 acres of land that was $8,000 as a down payment, and now I owe $20,000 more than I did to begin with?"

She said, "Yes, the interest is $300 a month."

It was a swindle. I said, "Well, that's it, I can't afford to live here no more." I gave up the property at the same time I left Louise, and I moved into town.

DONNIE

I TALKED TO DONNIE ONE MORE TIME. I was talking with my mom on the telephone one day. I'd left a bunch of stuff with her, so I called up and said, "Mom, I'm going to send you some money. I want you to go ahead and send me my coin collection and the other stuff I left in Worcester."

She got real quiet. I thought she had hung up. I said, "Mom? Mom?"

She answered me, "Yes."

I said, "I want to send you about $100. That should cover the extra stuff out there. Would you do that for me?"

She said, "I can't."

I said, "Why not? Why can't you?"

She didn't want to tell me, but she finally said, "Donnie spent your whole coin collection and pawned your stuff."

I said, "What?"

He was addicted to heroin, as I figured. She told me she woke up one night and heard all this noise. He was trying to rip the bathroom sink out of the wall. She tried to stop him and he broke her nose. I asked her, "Is he there right now?"

She said, "Yes."

I said, "Put him on." I said to him, "You hit Mom? You really think you're a real tough guy. You broke Mom's nose? I don't care how long it takes, but I will see you again."

He said, "I'll whip your butt." (He always talked real tough when a couple of thousand miles separated us.)

I just told him, "You know, when I see you, I'm going to hurt you worse than you've ever been hurt in your life."

A few days later, he heard that I was heading to Massachusetts on a bus. Instead of staying with my mom and sister, he decided he'd go to California. He planned to take the bus. He told somebody, "But if Bob sees me on the bus, he'll stop the bus, get me off, and beat the hell out of me." I would have. If I had seen him, I would have yanked him off and thumped him good. He took a plane out to the West Coast. I was only going to be home for 30 days, so on the 31st day of my visit, he called my mom. He said he was taking a plane back to Massachusetts. I never saw him. I never talked to him again.

Donnie died in 1983. I was working outside at home and heard the phone ring. I answered the phone. It was Joni. She said, "I've got some bad news."

I said, "Mom?"

She said, "No, Donnie."

I always expected that call. I brought him out to California with me to get him off of that garbage. He just did not want to quit.

MOJAVE

LUCKILY, I GOT A JOB WITH THE COUNTY. I got to travel all over Mojave County. At that time it was the fifth largest county in the United States, not including counties in Alaska. I went to work up in the mountains. I ran a four-square-mile county park up in Cedar, Arizona. They gave me housing, and it was probably one of the best jobs I ever had. My cabin had a little living room, bedroom, bathroom, and kitchenette. At the top of the property were translators for the CIA and FBI. That section was closed off. Government agencies shot microwaves through the antennas that were there. It was a *no access* zone for visitors.

The park liked my work so much they moved me from Cedar to Hualapai to be park custodian. I was supervisor of the park, so I ran the whole property. We had 21 cabins to rent out, four recreation areas with cabanas, and big stone buildings. The place was constructed by the Civilian Conservation Corps boys during the Great Depression. There were over one thousand campsites in five or so areas with trails. The mountain elevation changed by 100 feet. I had a crew under me, but I was basically on call 24 hours a day. We had trails going up to the top. When they walked, people had to sign in and put down the estimated time they would sign out. We gave them two hours. If hikers didn't sign out in two hours, I grabbed a first aid kit and walkie-talkie and hiked up to the top of the mountain to check if the people were okay. Nine times out of ten, once they got up there, they decided to camp out. I told them something like, "Well, you should have sent somebody down and told us at the office. It's not that long of a hike, it's only about a 45-minute hike. You signed in and said you'd be checking out around eight o'clock." Many, many a night I had to hike up there and do that.

I had to scale the mountain at all hours. I learned a long time ago not to be afraid of the dark or to be afraid of being alone in the woods because I realized *I* was the scariest thing in the woods. Seriously, I was the scariest thing in the woods.

There were other times when we had bad lightning strikes. A tree would be on fire, and I'd have to hike up into the woods with an axe and a water pack on me to cut the tree down and put the fire out. I'd usually have it all out and completely dead by the time the forest service showed up to help. Eventually, we had our own fire department in the area. If a tree caught fire, I called them and said, "Yes, there's a fire here. Looks like a single tree. I'm going to go up and knock it down, and if I need help, I'll radio you." I'd climb the mountain and make the tree fall where I wanted it to. Then I'd get right on it.

One of my other duties was to kind of lecture. Northern Arizona University and other colleges brought classes up to learn about management. I was supposed to lecture the students for 40 minutes, but what I generally did was say something like, "I know I'm not good at giving a lecture, so why don't we just turn this into a question and answer day, and I'll answer your questions as best I can." They liked that. They'd ask me all kinds of questions and I'd answer.

I got to know all the local people. The mountain community was a very closed society, and the people would not sell their land. They were fussy about who they would allow to move in up there. If someone wanted to sell, the whole property owners association got involved. They liked me because I kept the park very clean. On my days off, I took garbage sacks and walked the road.

Then we had classes with the Bureau of Land Management. I took fire science through them. I took a year of psychology in the masses to help me deal with the public. Then I took the emergency medical technician (EMT) course and went for my state license. I had to work in the emergency room for 40 hours and attend an autopsy. I watched the autopsy of a guy who had been a career alcoholic. The doctor removed his brain and showed us that brain and part of a brain from a normal person. His brain was kind of a greenish-grayish color, almost brown. The normal brain was pinkish in color and had little tiny holes where the cerebral fluid ran through. They sliced it, and they showed us all the way through how big the alcoholic's holes were, the whole gamut, and said, "That's the alcohol." Every time you take a drink of alcohol, you destroy brain cells. Marijuana is bad, too. They taught me that a career alcoholic, even though he might be sober for a month, still has the talk. His speech is slurred because of the brain damage

Out of over one hundred people, only four of us passed the test. I almost thought I was taking a test to become a doctor. It was all medical questions and medical terms. A good thing was that when I went to school, the county paid. It was on my own time but free.

Our instructor worked with the state police and Department of Public Safety. He taught cardiopulmonary resuscitation (CPR). The guy had all kinds of awards and was a really good professor. The first time I went to his class, he said, "Okay, say you've got to go for a ride. Before you get your seat belt on, there's one thing you need to do. You need to remember this because it's very important. Always urinate before you ride in a car. Nine times out of ten, when you get into an automobile accident, your seatbelt's going to rupture your bladder. That creates the condition known as peritonitis. It's poisoning. It poisons your system, and it's a very hard infection to clear up."

I was like, "Man, that makes sense." Ever since then, any time I'm going for a ride, even if it's just to the store, I make sure I go to the bathroom first. That stuck with me. That was around 1977.

It was a really interesting class, and I learned a lot of life-saving skills from it. Actually, I saved a little girl's life. I was in a restaurant and a little girl started choking. Her mom hadn't cut the meat small enough and a piece lodged in her throat. The mom was running around in circles panicking and screaming, "What do I do? What do I do?" I picked up the little girl, put my arms around her, made a fist underneath her rib cage, and proceeded to do the Heimlich maneuver. A chunk of meat flew out of her mouth and across the room. She breathed again. After that, I was the little girl's hero. Every time she saw me in town, she'd come walk with me and hold my hand.

I loved the park job, but the problem was that it got too political. There were 21 different committees that had something to do with the park around then. It got to the point that I was spending half of my time down in town with these committees, and then they asked me, "Well, how come your work is falling behind?"

Yes, finally I blew up one day, and I said, "Because I'm down here all the time arguing with you SOBs. You're not letting me do my work." I started suffering from acid reflux and ulcers. Finally, I just couldn't handle it anymore, and I quit. At three o'clock in the morning, I packed up my stuff. That morning I went down to see my boss, turned in my keys, apologized, and left. I had so much comp time, though, my checks lasted almost six months. I had hardly ever taken a day off, and I worked much more than eight hours a day. I worked a lot of sixteen-hour days.

LIL

I MET LIL IN THE MOUNTAINS AT HUALAPAI. She hiked a lot up there and we got to be real good friends. We used to go to the little diner nearby to have a cup of coffee. Lil was about six years older than I was. We hit it off, so we started dating. Lil and I went into business together and owned a bar in Kingman.

I quit drinking when I owned the bar in Kingman. I'd run it Friday night, all day Saturday, Saturday night, and close it at midnight. We opened up again at noon on Sundays. I'd go in on Sunday mornings to wash and wax the bar down to get the place ready, and there would be people sitting on the porch shaking and saying, "Hey, hurry up and open. I need a drink."

I'd say, "Well, I don't open until noon. You're just going to have to wait."

I remember looking at those people and realizing that one day, if I kept drinking like I was drinking, I was going to be sitting out there with them. Plus, I never got the picture of that alcoholic's brain out of my mind. I quit just like that. I drank beer, but beer never did anything for me. I just liked the taste of it, but I never got drunk on beer. I quit bourbon and all whiskey. I was a whiskey drinker. I chased Wild Turkey 150 proof with Old Crow and 7-up. Then I got into a Kessler kick and drank Kessler and Coke for a while. Then Platte Valley Corn Whiskey. I liked Platte Valley. It came in an old-time jug that you put up over your shoulder. It had XXX on it. I loved moonshine, too.

My wife's uncle, Uncle Lambert, looked like the guy on the Kellogg's Corn Flakes box that holds a pitchfork and has his wife with him, the one based after the American Gothic painting. Uncle Lambert had a still in his garage. He put shag carpeting in his garage to muffle the noise so people couldn't tell, but he kept getting busted for his still. Eventually, he hid that still somewhere else. He made the best moonshine. The first time I met him we went over to his ranch in Oklahoma. It was a hot summer day, hot and muggy. I said, "Have you got any water?"

He said, "Yes, I got some in a jar on the counter."

I said, "That's good." I figured, at least it's not tap water. I poured a big glass and I chugged it down. Well, it was moonshine. I thought I was going to die at first. It was like a flame came out of me, but it was good. I liked it. Every year, he'd send me a couple pints of it through the mail, UPS. Every year.

I had a good time running that bar. Once, I killed a six-foot coon tail rattler. I brought him to the bar and I skinned him out. I cut the meat up into sections, and I deep fried it. He was big enough to produce a couple of platters of fried rattlesnake. I set him on the bar. The bar was crowded. Everybody was going over and grabbing it. Somebody finally asked, "What kind of meat is this?"

I said, "It's rattlesnake."

A bunch of customers said, "What?"

I said, "Yes, rattlesnake," and then people flipped out. Almost everybody in the bar ran outside, and lots of them tried to make themselves throw up. It just made me laugh. The other guy and I stayed and finished off both platters of the meat.

He said, "You sure you took the poison out?"

I said, "They're not poisonous. From the head, you cut down about four inches, and you get rid of the poison gland. As long as the snake hasn't bitten himself, you're all right."

Sometimes they will bite themselves if you trap them and won't let them off pavement. The heat drives them crazy, and they strike themselves. You don't want to eat that snake meat because it's got poison through the whole body. In fact, my Indian friends would catch them and sling them around and around. Finally, they would snap the snakes like you would snap a whip. That would pop the heads right off of the snakes.

I had a few friends who were American Indians. They were Hopi, Navaho, and Apache. Arizona is known as an Indian state. There are a lot of reservations in Arizona. The Indians would come into town to do their grocery shopping, but mostly they stayed on their reservations. There were a lot of white people they didn't get along with. There was a lot of prejudice among whites and Indians both; at least that was my experience back in 1971.

People also told me blacks weren't welcomed in Kingman. In fact, there was only one black person who lived in Kingman at that time. She was an elderly woman who cleaned the doctors' offices. That's the only reason she was allowed to stay. One time before I got there—this was related to me from people I knew—there was a big community of black people down there. They were having a wedding one time, and an argument broke out. Someone called the police. Well, the cops came down, and they all got into a brawl. The police ran the all blacks out. It was quite a fight between the blacks and the white police officers. I don't know what they were fighting about.

I appreciated the different cultures. For example, I used to eat nothing but Mexican food. The first time I had it was when I moved to Big Sur. A Mexican guy and his wife worked at the lodge, and they invited me over for dinner one night. She cooked traditional Mexican food. She put out the vegetables, and she put out a bowl of chips and a big bowl of salsa. Then she brought us out our burritos and enchiladas. Eddie was taking his stuff and just covering it up with the salsa.

I said, "Must be good stuff." I covered my food with the salsa.

He said, "You better try that first. That's hot."

I said, "Really? Okay." I got a spoonful and ate it. I liked it. I said, "That's not too hot for me." I just poured it on.

He said, "You're the only gringo I know who can eat this stuff."

I just wolfed it down, and I just fell in love with Mexican food. I liked it hot, too. I never got sick. I never had an upset stomach. When I started back eating American food, I got acid reflux. I liked Mexican food so much I learned how to cook it. I made my own burritos and enchiladas. I don't like tacos, but I like chimichangas.

FLAGSTAFF

LIL AND I LEFT KINGMAN. She wanted to leave, and I was tired of running the bar. We shut it down and headed toward Colorado. On the way, we stopped in Flagstaff and decided to spend a few days there and check it out. I had only driven straight through it before and had never really looked around. We started driving around, and we liked it so much we decided to stay. That was in 1978. I wound up living there for almost 30 years.

When we first got to Flagstaff, we went to this store, and it was owned by the Babbitt brothers. At the time Bruce Babbitt was the governor of Arizona, and he was later the Secretary of the Interior under Bill Clinton. He and his brother Paul owned a lot of companies in Arizona.

We were in their family's store Babbitt Brothers, Lil and I. The place was full of Mormons and Lil was a died-in-the-wool atheist. She didn't want to hear anything about God. I believed in Jesus, but I hadn't accepted him as my savior. I guess my mom had put some basic beliefs in me. Lil and I were walking around in the store, and a clerk kept staring at me kind of funny. Finally, she came up to me and said, "Excuse me, sir. I hate to bug you for a second."

I said, "What's on your mind?"

She said, "Well I need to tell you something."

I said, "What's that?"

She said, "Well, the Holy Spirit's telling me to tell you something."

I say, "What's that?"

She said, "Jesus loves you. He really loves you."

I thought, *Wow*. Lil exploded. She wanted to get the girl fired and wanted to physically fight her. I finally had to tell her, "Lil, be quiet, the lady wasn't talking to you. She was talking to me."

She was like, "Do you like that, what's she's saying about *Jesus*?"

I said, "Yes, I do. I do. For some reason, I do." It was humbling. Many years later, I realized I was about to go down the most cynical path of my life when the lady said that to me, and right at the start Jesus was telling me that He loved me. That made quite a difference when I hit rock bottom, the difference between life and death.

Before we got completely settled there in Flagstaff, I went home to Worcester, Massachusetts, to visit Mom and Joni. Joni was living at a commune called Harold House and Mom was doing okay. During that month I got saved, or at least I thought I did. That girl at the store in Flagstaff made an impression, but it wasn't God's time. He was working on me, for sure. I basically made a decision, and it felt like the road I needed to go down, but it didn't stick. When I left Worcester, I drove cross-country back to Flagstaff. My faith didn't even make it to the Grand Canyon. I started doing things I shouldn't have been doing. I started doing drugs again. When we went to Flagstaff and that girl told me Jesus loves me, that was at the beginning of the most evil part of my life.

Lil and I went to Vegas all the time, gambling and partying. One time we were up there and just decided to get married. We'd been living together for, I think, three years, four years, so we figured we'd make it legal.

Back in Flagstaff I started doing carpentry work and we bought a house up on Lake Mary Road for $22,000. We only put $5,000 down. Those were the days. The payments were $200 a month and it was a seven-year loan, so it wouldn't take long to pay off. Lil and I did all of our exploring at night. For a year, we roamed Flagstaff in the dark. After that, we decided to start checking the town out during the day, and we were blown away by the things we had driven by all those nights and had never seen. Like different parts of Lake Mary and Mormon Lake.

The wildlife in Flagstaff was cool. When I first moved to Flagstaff, there were two maulings by bears. One happened when a family had pulled up alongside the road, the main highway, I-17, coming up from Phoenix. They put their sleeping bags right off the road. The dad woke up and heard rustling around in the ice chest. A black bear was going through their stuff. The dad threw a boot at the bear, and the bear turned on his son. His son was in a sleeping bag and it mauled his son bad, but he lived. The guy got up and hit the animal with sticks and rocks, and the bear finally took off. Another time, a lady was out hanging clothes on her clothesline. She lived outside of town. A sow and cubs showed up, and the lady was between the cubs and their mama. She yelled at her little boy—he was three or four years old—to get in the house and lock the door. The bear attacked. She lost her legs, but she lived. Here in New Hampshire, I saw a bear a while back. He ran across Route 4. I bet he was 400 pounds. He stood straight up and was at least as tall as I am.

The country in Flagstaff is like New England. We were up around 7,000 feet, so we had four seasons. What was cool about it was that if we got tired of the sights, we drove ten minutes down the hill and were back in the desert. I remember swimming in January. Lil and I had a pet skunk and a pet raccoon. The skunk we named Lulu after my first wife. I bought it from a pet shop for $75. It was de-scented and had all its shots. So did the raccoon. Skunks are blind and can see only about six inches, but they have a good sense of smell. Lulu liked to chew my legs. She sat in my lap and purred like a cat. Skunks are members of the mustelid family, which are close to the cat family. I always knew if she wanted to spray me. She would stomp her front feet and turn her body into a U shape. Once the tip of the tail comes up, watch out! She couldn't spray though, so it was funny when she got mad.

One day I came home from work and Lil was all upset about something. I said, "What's the matter?"

She said, "Nothing. Will you go out and feed Lulu?"

I said, "Yes, you didn't feed her yet?"

She said, "I think something's wrong. I took her food, but Lulu didn't come right out."

Well, I went out to the pen and saw the bowl of food and there was Lulu running around the pen. Well, then came the real Lulu out of the den (I had made an underground den for her). The first Lulu was a wild skunk that had seen the real Lulu and wanted to breed with her. Lil came out to see and got mad. She said, "Earlier, that skunk was out of the pen and I thought it was Lulu escaped, so I hit it in the butt with a broom. I'm amazed I didn't get sprayed!."

The raccoon was Rachel and she was very, very smart. I got her when she was six weeks old. Raccoons will only take up with one to two people. They'll never take up with anybody else. If anybody else tries to get close, the raccoons stand up on their hind legs, walk on their back legs toward you with their arms up in the air, and hiss, showing their teeth. I liked Rachel, but there was no keeping her once spring came. I had her a good pen. It was a double pen that went underground, just like Lulu's. I had to seal Lulu's so she couldn't tunnel her way out because skunks will do that. Well, raccoons will get out above ground, so when I built Rachel's pen, I had chicken wire and I went down the sides with baling wire and pliers. I was tightening every joint and I looked behind me. Sure enough, Rachel was following me and undoing the baling wire quicker than I was tightening it up. I knew there was no keeping her then. She escaped, and we didn't see her for a couple of months. Then one day she showed up on the edge of the property. She had four little baby raccoons with her. She chattered away when she saw me. She got to see me and I got to look at her babies. I didn't come near her. They ran back into the woods. She just wanted to show me her family.

Well, with Lulu, we were going to let her breed. You have to let her hibernate to breed. Some neighbor kid got a BB gun for Christmas. He knew that I had a trap door on her den and he lifted it up and he filled her full of ball bearings. There were some punks up there.

We also had a little dog. This guy came down in his truck and deliberately drove on our property and tried to run over Lil's little dog. I saw it happen. I thought, *All right then*. I waited an hour, and then I went driving around the neighborhood. Sure enough there was the same truck, parked. That night I went back over there. I didn't want to kill anybody, but I wanted to make my point. I popped off the dust cap on the front wheel, took off the pin that holds your wheel on, and I loosened the nut up on the passenger's side so he'd go off of the road and not into traffic.

I put the cap back on it. The next day on my way to town, I saw the truck off in a ditch. There was a tow truck trying to get it out. I just drove by and beeped the horn and waved to him. He knew it was me, but he also knew not to start anything he couldn't finish.

That was nothing, though. I had taken a break from motorcycles until I moved to Flagstaff, but as soon as we were settled there, I got back into biker culture big time. I had all the gear and was soon immersed in the life. Even so, God was trying hard to get to me.

Christmas brought back a lot of sadness. One year when we were little, we were living with my aunt. My mom and my aunt got in a big fight on Christmas Eve, so Mom grabbed us kids and we left. It being close to the end of the month, she didn't have any money. We just walked toward town as she tried to figure out what she could do for us for Christmas dinner. A friend of hers was driving by. He saw us and pulled over. I guess he figured out what was going on because he took us to the Waldorf cafeteria in Worcester and bought us Christmas dinner.

Lil and I had a friend who worked with the Arizona Department of Economics. Her name was Carrie. Every year, Carrie told us about a single-parent family and found out all the sizes and needs that they had. Lil and I would spend about $2,000 on them. We bought clothes, shoes, food, toys, and other stuff. We would sneak over Christmas Eve and unload everything on the porch or at the door, even a Christmas tree with some decorations on it. Then I would bang on the door and Lil and I would run and hide. It never failed. Children always answered the door. They would say, "Mama! Santa Claus came!"

Jesus was working on me in every way imaginable. I was just too drugged up and wild and busy to notice. I was almost electrocuted once. I think Jesus was trying to get to me one big accident at a time, but I was too stubborn to listen. One day I was fixing our hot water heater. I thought I was smart. I capped off the wires and had them taped up against the wall so I wouldn't touch them. I kept the electricity on while I worked on the thing. Well, I forgot that in old houses the electricity is often grounded through the water pipes. When disconnecting the union, I was sitting in a puddle of water. All of a sudden, I've got 220 volts running through me. I couldn't let go of the pipes and my wife was yelling, "What's wrong? What's wrong?" I couldn't even talk. It blew the main fuse that was below the meter. I had 440 volts coming into the meter. They split there between a fuse on one side and a blank on the other. So, 220 volts were going into the house, which hit the breaker box and split again into 110s. I was sitting there in a puddle and my back was burning. Finally, I was somehow, miraculously, able to let go of it. My hands were burned, my butt was burned, and I was wedged up against the hot water heater and the wall. The heat gave me a headache right away, and I had to lie down for a little while. That was a close call.

HAVASUE

LIL AND I QUIT WORKING. Our accountant told us we had to take a year off from work. We had made too much money and our investments were paying off too well. Anything we would have earned at our jobs would have cost us a lot in taxes, so we took a year off. Man, we made a lot of money together. We were millionaires at one point. We were worth about $2 million. It was all legal.

We bought a houseboat on Lake Havasu. We took our ski boat down there and bought a fourteen-foot aluminum boat with a seven-and-a-half horsepower motor. We also had a Murphy Jet wee boat with a 454 engine that for a while was the fastest boat on Lake Havasu. It did 75 miles an hour. Lil skied barefoot behind it. We fished all over that lake. We camped a lot on the smaller lakes. There are over a thousand miles of shoreline in Arizona, including all of the lakes and the rivers and everything else, and a lot of those are good trout spots. At the time, you couldn't have a gasoline engine, so we had an electric engine and two Diehard batteries. We charged them up to last a weekend at a time. We got to the lake on Thursday nights and fished all day Friday, Saturday, and most of Sunday. When the batteries got low, I hooked jumper cables up to the front of my truck and set the batteries on the fender. You never want to put the batteries on the ground to charge them because the ground just draws everything out of them.

We used to invite all of our friends down from California and Flagstaff for Memorial Day weekend. Lil and I went to the lake a week ahead to set up a good camping spot because if you waited until Memorial Day weekend (even as early as Wednesday) you couldn't find any space. Lil and I looked for a spot that was, as we called it, "rattlesnake free." Usually, it was a beach. I could sit there and catch five and six-pound bass from my lawn chair. There was great fishing on Havasu until the government put stripers in the water, which killed all the bass.

VERDE

LIL AND I RAFTED THE VERDE RIVER 80 MILES. We rafted from Camp Verde to Rome. Locals call it the Green River because *verde* is the Spanish word for green. At one time, Camp Verde over in Texas was an outpost. Before the Civil War and railroads were built in Arizona, the United States Secretary of War Jefferson Davis started a program for using camels in the American Southwest, so the Army went to the Middle East and brought back camels. They drove the pack up from New Mexico to the Colorado River and to Fort Mohave in Arizona, which was down around where Bullhead City is now. They sent camels up to Kingman to Fort Beale, and then they sent them on down to Camp Verde in Texas. I think there was another base of them down in Tucson. They figured the camels could haul more on less water than mules and horses could.

Weird laws came into being. I read some of them once. It was illegal to let your camels spit on the sidewalks on Sundays, and if your camels messed in the street, you had to clean it up, immediately. Camels are nasty animals. They cough up this slime looking stuff that stinks and they'll spit it at you. They'll try to pee on you. They're really nasty. That spit is the size of a softball.

I knew where all the old forts were, and I toured them. There are no actual rooms, but there are foundations where the buildings were. I took my metal detector and checked all over Fort Beale. I found U.S. Cavalry buttons, horseshoes, and old horseshoe nails. Then I went down to Fort Mohave and found much the same thing. At Camp Verde, not only did I find buttons, but I also found a belt buckle and an old metal part of a canteen. I had a bunch of old U.S. Cavalry buttons made of brass, but they were green because they had been lying out there for a long time.

Army payroll used to travel the mountains between Kingman and Bullhead City. The troops got paid every few months—in cash unless they were on an allotment system—with gold double eagles and other coins. The privates made about thirteen dollars a month I think. One day, this sergeant and a couple of privates in charge of carrying the payroll got ambushed by Indians halfway across Golden Valley about where my ranch was. They got shot up bad, and there were two of them left. The wounded sergeant and soldier made it up into the mountains outside of Kingman. The story is that they found a cave, put the payroll in the cave, and covered up the entrance with rocks, and that's where they made their last stand. The Indians killed them, and no one ever found the payroll, the sergeant's body, or the last trooper's body. They found the other two bodies mutilated. The story is that Apaches that had traveled up North raided them.

There were Apaches who had a reservation down by Havasu. In the five years before I moved to Kingman in '71, so it was about '66, this man and his son were up in those mountains camping out. They had a metal detector and hiked the mesas and supposedly found the cave. They found an old .44 caliber Navy Colt, a Walker Colt. It was the side arm that the dragoons used. Even better, they found sacks of gold coins. They took one gold double eagle out. They brought it to the chamber of commerce and right away everyone asked, "Where did you find this?" It spooked the man and his son.

He just said, "Well, we found it up in the mountains."

The others asked, "Where about? Do you remember where?"

The man said, "We could try to find it again." The government people and the man looked for two days. I think that they deliberately didn't show them where it was because the government would have seized it all. It was government property, supposedly army payroll. They never did find it and as far as anybody knows, it's still up in there. The story is that the cave was beside Secret Pass, which was a trail the Spanish used when they would come up from Mexico. They had missions in New Mexico, California, and Texas, like The Alamo.

The Spanish Catholics tried to indoctrinate the Pueblos. They destroyed their sacred items and forced their religion and rules on the Indians. In 1680 one of the Pueblo medicine men, Pope, started a big revolt. All the Pueblo Indians and some Apaches rose up and killed a bunch of the Spanish (400, including lots of priests) and sent the rest packing to Spain.

They left all their cattle and horses there, and that's why there were so many wild horses and cattle in the area. The horses weren't native to North America. They were completely unmanaged and so they reproduced. After a hundred years there were huge horse herds down in Texas, Arizona, New Mexico, and Southern California. After the Civil War many a rancher got his start by going out and rounding up longhorn cattle. They branded them and sold them. That's how John Chisum and several other big ranchers got their starts. They quickly tried to ice everybody else out of the deal. If they caught somebody rounding up wild cattle, they'd hang them. Rustlers and ranchers battled through several range wars. John Wayne played the rancher in the 1970 movie *Chisum.*

I like movies about the Old West. The earliest Alamo movie was made in 1905. It was a silent movie in black and white. In that one, they made Mrs. Dickinson, Captain Dickinson's wife, the heroine of the Alamo. She was one of the few survivors. She and her daughter and a couple of other women and children were the only survivors. John Wayne directed his own version of The Alamo. He starred in it as Davy Crockett. His production company spent millions to make it. They built an Alamo set in Texas with a mission, corrals, wells, everything. They started in the late '50s, but it wasn't released until around '62. They hoped to win an Oscar, and they didn't win. They were considered for seven different Oscars, but they didn't win a single Oscar for it. He only won one Oscar in his lifetime and that was when he was older. He won an Oscar for best actor in *True Grit* in 1970. It was the only Oscar he ever won, and he was in well over one hundred movies.

STORM

WE HAD LOTS OF EXCITEMENT WHEREVER WE WENT. I guess you could say we lived in what was still the Wild West. I was in more tornadoes in Arizona. One spring, I had just gotten my income tax refund check, so I went over to a truck stop where a buddy of mine worked. He was going to cash the check for me. Three tornadoes hit, and by the time I got home, one had peeled the whole roof off my house. Radar tracked three of them touching down in the vacant lots across the street from my house. Another time I was out at Lake Havasu. For Memorial Day weekend, we rented a 35-foot patio boat, like a pontoon boat. It was about ten o'clock at night and we went on a boat ride. It was dark out, but we had flashlights and lights on the boat. Well, suddenly the water got really rough with big waves. We couldn't figure out why. The wind was blowing. The waves were crazy high. We pulled into Black Meadow Landing, and a huge wave picked us up and put us down on top of the dock. We slid the boat off the dock and headed back to camp. The waves were breaking over the front of the boat and getting all the way back to me, the driver. The waves were waist-high. I set her wide open, turned around a corner into the cove, and the wind and waves lifted us up on one pontoon! We were going so fast that the boat lifted out of the water and landed hard on the beach. We had a heck of a time getting that boat back into the water, but we got it there. One lady who was with us became hysterical. She jumped under the concrete picnic table, and my wife had to slap her a couple of times to calm her down. At about three in the morning the coast guard and the rangers came by. One asked, "Is everybody okay here?"

I said "Yes, what was that storm that hit?"

He said, "There were three tornadoes on the lake."

I said "When?"

He said, "Around midnight."

I said, "We were on the lake at midnight."

He said, "Well, you're lucky to be alive because they were right on this lake right outside of where you're camping here."

102

Three tornadoes. We never saw a one of them. All I remember seeing with our flashlights and the boat lights were the waves coming over the bow of the boat. I thought it was just a windstorm or something that had kicked up the waves. If I had known we had tornadoes, I would have beached the boat anywhere and forgotten about getting back to camp.

POT

LIL AND I SMOKED POT. We weren't selling, though. When we moved to Flagstaff, we brought a quarter pound of Red Hair and a full pound of Colombian Gold with us. That was our only stash. Then at one point, we had a grow house. In our cabin, we let the pot take over the whole upstairs. We lined the floors and walls in layers and layers of really thick plastic. I put in a foot of topsoil. I went down to the desert and brought back desert sand. I had to sterilize it, so I baked it at 425 degrees for about 30 minutes. That killed any insects and spider mites in the sand. If insects and spider mites get in your house plants your plants start turning yellow and the leaves shrivel. I also baked the potting soil. Then I mixed the sand and soil together. It didn't take all that long to grow the first crop. The room was maybe twelve by twenty feet. We had starter beds. We germinated the seeds and got the plants started. When they got a few inches high, we pulled the ones we didn't want and tossed them. We had one artificial grow light in there for ultraviolet and then a regular fluorescent light because that gives off infrared, and you need both to grow marijuana. We also had misters that would go on and off at certain times. I installed little rubber hose water lines that went to each one of the plants. We set the thermostat so it never got cooler than 60 degrees when the lights were off. It would get up around 90 degrees when all the grow lights were buzzing, and a fan blew a gentle breeze to circulate the air. Everything was rigged up with timers. We put nightcrawlers in the soil because they make good fertilizer. Of course, we liked to fish a lot, so we saved three dollars a dozen on worms. We just went upstairs, pulled out a can full of nightcrawlers, and went fishing.

Only two other people knew we had the grow house. We trusted those two people completely. We kept a big padlock on it. Lil and I had to go to Los Angeles every couple of months for a week and take care of business, so we needed someone to come in every day and top the plants. We told the guys, "Whatever you top is yours." You have to cut the tips so the plants will branch out. Those plants were so healthy they grew up into the lights. There were 21 fingers on a leaf, and the fingers were wide. We did not sell straight out. Sometimes friends came by and said, "You know where to score something?"

I'd say, "I might be able to help you, if you give me a few days." Only for friends, we processed pot and sold it to them, but they thought it came from somewhere else. Lil and I picked a bunch of tops and dried them out. We had a special way to do that so the pot didn't look homegrown. Even what we smoked, ourselves, never looked homegrown. We knew better because if you got busted with marijuana, the police could tell right away if it was homegrown, and they'd track down the grower. Here's how you do it. You put the tips in a baggy, like a plastic sandwich bag. You fill the baggy up and then you seal it and you squish it and squish it and then set it, with the baggy full, on top of the lights. The heat draws the condensation, so the pot gets real wet. You keep squishing it. You throw a few seeds in there and add food coloring. Eventually, ours looked like Mexican pot, but it was much stronger than anything you could get on the streets. After about three days, we poured it into a pan and set the pan on the lights. That dried out the weed. Three days after that, we bagged it up again, weighed it to an ounce, and added a little more for friends. The price on the streets was about $50 for a quarter ounce.

Friends would ask, "Where'd you get this?"

We'd say, "Well, we know people. It just takes them a while to get it to us."

We had to charge them, so they would believe the pot wasn't ours. I kept a lot of plants going and managed the light cycle so they never went to seed. We did all that for over three years, and our plants never went to seed. Lil took a picture of me standing in the middle of those pot trees, and all you can see is part of my beard and one of my eyes. I'm completely covered with green all the way down.

I learned how to do all that by studying agriculture for a year at Clark University back in Worcester. I figured pot must be one of the easiest plants to grow because it's a weed. I just put the things I had learned about other plants into growing pot. I read some books on it, and I found out what things to watch out for, like what chemicals you don't use. We didn't use insecticide. At one point, we got spider mites. I tried the old soapy water trick, but it didn't kill them. Finally, I called the nursery down the road, and I said, "Yeah, I've got some plants, and they've got spider mites real bad. I don't want to use insecticides on them because they're edible plants."

The lady on the phone asked me, "Well, what kind of plants are they?"

I said, "Well, they're plants."

Right away she knew, but she was cool. She said, "Oh, I get you. I get you." She said, "Here's what you try. Take some cayenne pepper and mix it up with water and spray them with the cayenne pepper."

That didn't work, so I wound up using malathion. I had a friend who was an exterminator, and he said the safest insecticide to use is malathion because it breaks down in ultraviolet and infrared light within two weeks. He told us not to smoke anything for about two months to give the malathion plenty of time to break down. So, before we sprayed, we cut a bunch of tops to hold us over. The chemical killed all the spider mites, but it also killed all the nightcrawlers.

During that year off, Atari had just come out, so we bought the console and controls and 40 different games. Lil and I smoked pot and played games all night long. We slept during the day. We'd go out and get something to eat in the evening after dark, go for a ride for a while, roll a couple joints, and drive up and down the road smoking and checking out the area in the dark. We were just night people. We liked nights. It was cooler at night, so summer was a good time to explore. We slept on an air mattress in front of the TV in the living room. That was good in winter because the wood stove was right there. We kept the stove cranked up in the winter. It made it so hot in there that I'd have to go outside in February and sit because I was sweating. We got below zero, but in the house it would be 100 degrees. Everybody joked that we were vampires because they never saw us during the day. Then, finally, we started coming out once we figured out how awesome Flagstaff was during the day. After about three years, we got burned out on the garden upstairs, so we decided to tear it up. We broke off the branches and filled up two big lawn and leaf garbage sacks, the big green garbage ones, all the way full. The stems were so thick I had to saw them. Even though it was hot outside, I got a fire going and burned the branches. I didn't want anything left over. I took out all the soil. We cleaned the upstairs, took the plastic off the walls, and turned the space into two bedrooms.

WORK

I WENT TO WORK FOR A CINDER BLOCK FACTORY. It was just supposed to be a temporary job through an agency, but the factory liked my work so much they paid the fees to hire me outright from the temporary agency and made me assistant manager in the plant. Because I knew how to do maintenance, they probably thought, *Oh, we have a mechanic* and *an electrician.* I was able to do repairs on the machines when they broke down, but I also had other foremen come over and do it.

I rebuilt one of their machines, a block-splitting machine, and they were so impressed with that they made me the foreman. They were having a lot of problems with the block construction. Of all the blocks they made, only about ten percent were good enough to use. The rest just crumbled. They were sand blocks, and they had to be split. My first job there was to split every one of those blocks. That was when I first got hired. The splitting machine they had was so messed up that they were getting, out of a whole pallet of blocks, only three or four that would split right. The rest were rejects. So, I took over. For state contracts, each block had to withstand pressure of 80,000 pounds per square inch. I started tinkering with the equipment. I used a vibrator and everything else I could think of and finally got the blocks to where they wouldn't crumble until they had over 200,000 pounds per square inch. The factory was able to get quite a few more contracts, and I cut the rejects down to less than one percent.

As a matter of fact, every year the company had a reject sale in the fall and donated all the money to 4H. It had been going on for years, and one year, because our equipment worked so much better, we didn't have enough blocks, so my boss had me run some seconds. I'd go to work at six in the morning, and I wouldn't get home until eight or nine o'clock at night. I worked long, long days, but we had so many contracts in the summer, and when the blocks started coming out so high quality, we got a lot more contracts. Whatever the number was, we made it. My bosses were blown away.

I quit that job when an 8,000-pound motor fell on my shoulder. That was in 1983, I think. A guy at the block plant jumped down into a silo. I said, "You need to go out there to the sand silo. There's a pipe that's going into the sand. You just bust it loose." I told him to get up on the edge of the silo because the sand was wet, so it was coming out the bottom. It was heavy. Well, he thought he knew better, so he jumped into the middle of it. Immediately, he got sucked right down to where the augers were. Lucky for him, I always made sure there was a spotter. The spotter hit the panic button, and we shut everything down. The guy was buried up to his neck. I went running up the stairs. We had an 8,000-pound electric motor hanging in there, and for no reason it fell just as I ran under it. It hit my shoulder. My reflexes were a lot better back then. I was able to run out from under it in a hurry, but it hurt big time. I didn't think anything of it. We got the guy out of there, got him into an ambulance, and they took him to a hospital and checked him out. He was okay. I wound up having to fire him.

The next morning when I woke up, I couldn't lift myself out of the bed like normal. My left arm was paralyzed. For the next two and a half years, it was curled up like I'd had a stroke or had multiple sclerosis or something. At one point it turned black and was shriveled to less than half the normal size around. I saw 28 doctors. The last four doctors I saw wanted to amputate my arm because it was black, and they thought it was making my shoulder worse. I said, "No, you're not cutting off my arm."

They said, "Well, it's dead."

I said, "Well then, you know what you do? You get in there and take out anything that's going to stink. Then put hinges on it and rig a string up to my thumb so I can hold my beer. You're not cutting off my arm."

Some of the tests they did should be illegal. I finally saw a doctor who was a cardiovascular surgeon. He took one look at all the test results and said, "I know exactly what this is."

I said, "What is it? You're better than the other 27 doctors?"

He said, "When that motor hit you, it compressed your clavicle to your top rib, and it severed your motor nerve. It also damaged your spine because the MRI showed damage to your spine. What I'm going to do is go into your armpit, collapse your lung, move your lung out of the way, move your heart out of the way, and go up ahead and remove your top rib. Then, my partner, he's a neurosurgeon, he's going to step in. He's going to try to reattach the nerve. No guarantees, though."

I said, "All right. Go for it."

They had me in an induced coma for about a week, and at one point, I think it was three days into the coma, the doctors called my family up at around three in the morning and said, "You better get over here. Bob's lungs are filling up with blood, and we think we're going to lose him." So they came over. I didn't know anything about it, and they didn't tell me that for about six months after I got out of the hospital.

Once I was okay the doctors kept me there in the hospital for about three weeks. Before the surgery, I had told the surgeon that I wanted my rib and anything he took off my spine. He said, "Why? You can't have that."

I said, "Let's get something straight, doc. That's not your property. It's my property. It's my body, and I want the pieces of it because when I die I want to have all the pieces together." I have saved all my teeth. I've pulled most of my teeth myself. Believe it or not, the surgeon handed me those pieces of bone as I was leaving the hospital.

FIREWOOD

WE CUT OUR OWN FIREWOOD. I kept about ten cords in the yard plus a bunch of big rounds. After my arm surgery I went to therapy for a couple of years. I got really good at squeezing the tennis ball, but nobody was hiring tennis ball squeezers anywhere. I was tired of not working, so I started selling firewood and making good money doing it. I bought a twenty-pound splitting maul. I took the handle off and welded a solid steel one into it. Seven days a week, I split firewood from before the sun came up in the morning until after sundown.

I had friends who would drop off all these big rounds, and I'd say, "Yes, I'll split it for you for free. I need the exercise." I did that for a couple of years, plus our own, and then decided, "Hey, there's good money in firewood, and I know where to get it." I went and I got a commercial license to cut it. We invested $5,000 into the business. I ran half a dozen chainsaws, got three brand new chains for each one, and bought electric shock guard kits. I fixed my truck up with overload ability and air suspension. I had coil and leaf springs, too. I pulled a trailer that held a cord and a half. My truck would hold a cord and if I stacked the wood right, I could haul three cords total with the truck and the trailer.

I was hauling up to Cambridge for $125 a cord. In Phoenix I got $165 a cord. To haul it over to Indio, California, we earned $275 a cord. Lil and I would no sooner pull into Indio to deliver, and people would start running out of their houses to stop us in the road. The law wouldn't let you cut firewood in California. The government passed a moratorium on it. There were just too many people, and not many wilderness areas left. People had to import wood from Oregon, Washington State, Idaho, parts of Nevada, and other states. People stopped us in the middle of the street to hire us. They would say, "Where are you going with that?"

I'd say, "This wood is already sold."

They'd say, "What have you got in there?"

I'd say, "Three cords."

They'd say, "I'll give you $ 1,500."

I always answered them, "I wish I could, but I promised somebody else. Write down your name for me, and I can be back over in a week or two weeks. I'll bring you three cords at $1,500 bucks."

They'd say, "Yes, okay, do you want the money now?"

Then I'd say, "No, we will bring it over. If you change your mind and don't want it, I'm not worried about it." About ten people would stop me on every trip into California.

We always took Mondays off. Every Tuesday I went out and found a huge pine tree. I usually had to make six cuts to get it to fall down. Once the tree was lying on the ground, it was still over my head. That's how big those pines were. I cut eighteen-inch thick rounds and went from there. I got Lil a ten-inch chainsaw and a twelve-inch chainsaw. She did the branches and cut the logs to be eighteen inches long. We could cut a whole tree up in one day. We spent the next two days hauling it all home. We were way out in the middle of nowhere, so nobody knew what we were doing or heard us. I made a ramp so I could slide or roll those rounds up into the truck. I laid them sideways so half of them were touching the truck. I set the edge of the round on the bottom of the slide, then got down underneath it and could push and slide the round all the way into the truck bed. It blew Lil away. She said one time, "I've never seen anybody as strong as you." Those rounds were about 500 pounds. I could only haul six of them at a time. I drove six home, pushed them out into the yard, and then drove back into the woods for the next load. Lil's jobs were to cut off all the branches and keep me company. We usually got done around noon on Wednesday. Then I'd start splitting the wood. I had to split those big rounds with a hammer and wedges first. I split them in half and again, then put them in the logger. I sat on a round and just slid one piece at a time into the machine. About every fifteen minutes, I had to stop because the split pile would be so high in front of the machine. By the end of one day, the finished pile would be the size of a small living room and higher than my head. We made the $5,000 back the first year with a profit.

Then we spent Friday mornings delivering to customers in Flagstaff. I might make two or three runs down to Phoenix. We took cords over to Kingman to supply the lodge. We charged them only $65 a cord. I had a customer there who paid $125 per cord and he bought all I could bring him. Every weekend I'd bring three loads for him. He had a fire every day, even in summer. He liked to get up in the morning and build a fire in his fireplace and sit there drinking his coffee staring at the fire all day. Then he'd come down to the bar and hang out, get a sandwich, then drink his beer. Then he'd go back home and build a fire, and he'd keep his fire going all night. He'd sit there drinking his beer and watching the fire. We had a lot of customers like him over there. We were always able to get rid of our firewood.

DIVORCE

OUR MARRIAGE LASTED FIVE YEARS. Lil had somebody, and I knew it. She would get up in the middle of the night, trying to be real quiet, and get dressed. I remember the last night, she stood to put her coat on and told me, "Bob, I really love you." She went out to go and be in somebody else's arms. I called her on it the next day.

I said, "Here's the way it's going to be. You can be with me, or you can be with him, but you can't be with both of us. You have to make up your mind. If you want to be with me, that's fine. I'll never throw it in your face. I'll never bring it up again, but you have to break it off clean with him because if I see you with him, I'm going to think the worst. If you want to be with him, more power to you. We'll have to stay friends because we have all this business together."

She said, "I want to be with you."

That conversation happened in the morning. I had started plowing roads all the way down to Oak Creek Canyon for the county. After we had that talk, I went on to work, and when I came home she wasn't there. That didn't mean anything because Lil always worked late. She had gotten a job with a cable television company. The office closed at four, but people were still there after that. The company just stopped answering the phone at closing time and let an answering machine record messages. Not long after I got home, Lil's mom called me and said, "It's an emergency. I've got to get a hold of Lil."

I said, "Well, she's probably down at the office, but she's not answering the phone." Lil's mom said she really needed to talk to Lil, so I said, "Okay. I'll run down and tell her to call you."

I got on my bike and I rode down to the cable company. Lil wasn't there. There was a store right next door and I knew the guy running the store. I asked him, "Did Lil just leave?"

He said, "No, she left at 3:30." This was after five.

I knew the guy she was messing around with, so I took a ride up by his house. Sure enough, her car was parked there. That was it. They saw me, and they went and hid out in the woods. I left. Lil called me about midnight and said, "We need to talk."

I said, "No. Actually, we don't need to talk. Come on and get all your stuff. You've made your decision. Now you're going to have to live with it. I'm not going to play second fiddle to anyone."

Not too long after that, Lil got in an accident on the guy's bike. They went off the road, hit a cement culvert, and flipped the bike. She got impaled on an iron rung on a telephone pole, one of the rungs technicians stand on. The metal bar went into her brain. The EMTs managed to keep Lil alive, but barely. Because we were still married, I had to give permission for doctors to fly her up to the Flagstaff hospital to the neurosurgeon. Doctors saved her, but she was dingy after that. They went down hard on that bike.

We got divorced. I had a code and lived by it all my life. I didn't mess around with married women or women who had boyfriends. One time back in Kingman, this girl named Edie who was a waitress started hitting on me and I said, "Hey, what are you doing? You're married. You've got a wedding band on."

She said, "No, I'm not married. I just wear that so guys in the restaurant won't hit on me. I'm single."

I took her out. Two days later, a guy I work with told me, "Edie's married. Her husband's my best friend. He's a really nice guy."

I said, "No, she's not married. She told me she's not married. She just wears a wedding band because she's a waitress."

"Well, it's true she's a waitress, but she is married."

She came to see me that day, and I said, "You lied to me. You made me break one of my main rules."

She said, "What's that?"

I said, "Messing around with somebody else's woman. Don't come back around me." She didn't want to go and she was crying. I said, "Don't. You're wasting your tears on me because I'm as cold as ice now."

HIT

I WAS HIT BY A TRUCK ONCE. About the time of the divorce, I started working for the Mojave County Road Department. I ran heavy equipment like semi-trailer trucks, dump trucks, snowplows, and that kind of machinery. It was rough and project jobsites were remote sometimes. It might take me an hour and a half to get up to the job site.

I had a semi run right over the top of me. His tractor didn't hit me, but his trailer hit the front of my truck and came down right over my head and crushed the roof in. I hurt my neck a little bit. Another time, I got hit by a one-ton produce box truck. I was plowing the roads in Flagstaff. I spotted him coming into the curb at a strange angle. The roads were pure ice. He was doing about 70 miles an hour when he hit that ice. He immediately started flying, hit the guardrail, bounced off, and headed my way. I set my plow down and set my air brake. My plan was to pull off the road, but I looked in the rearview mirror and there were maybe twenty cars behind me. They were following my plow. I knew then that if I pulled off the road, he was going to hit at least a dozen of those cars. He was going so fast. He hit my plow hard so hard he bent the frame of the big dump truck I was in. My body hit the steering wheel which cracked a bunch of ribs on the side of me that had the seatbelt across it. If I'd had on a shoulder harness, I wouldn't have even gotten hurt. He slid by me. As he rolled on by, I looked into his window. He had wild hair and his eyes were huge. His transmission and engine had come up through the floorboards on his box truck and they were sitting in front of him. He slid on past, did a couple of 360s, and finally stopped. I couldn't get out of the truck because the door was jammed. The highway patrol was there immediately.

Working that job, I travelled all over Mojave County and the Arizona strip, which is up where all the polygamists live. I spent a lot of time around Littlefield and Colorado City and all that land on the north side of the Grand Canyon up in there. The polygamists were very unsociable people; they just didn't trust outsiders. We went up there in the middle of the polygamy area two weeks every year to upgrade the

116

roads. We weren't allowed to stay in their towns. We had to stay up in Utah and drive down and work each day. What really gets me was, if I was walking on the sidewalk or through a store and said "Hi" to a family, the guy would just kind of look at me, and the ladies wouldn't make eye contact. They'd put their faces down and softly say something like, "Good day, sir," and walk away.

The children were totally hostile. I know that sounds strange, but the children were really hostile. That was because, in the '50s, the Mohave County Sheriff's Department went up there and arrested all of the adults for polygamy. A friend I worked with was the guy who drove the bus when the cops brought the families down to the county seat. The cops put the polygamists on trial, but they couldn't convict them because the polygamists were smart. No matter how many wives a man had, only one marriage was registered with the county, and all the rest were only in church records. The county wasn't allowed to seize the church records.

I'm not bragging, but I did a good job keeping the road open when I worked for the county. There were a lot of times when they would reroute traffic off of I-40 and I-17 down to 89A and on to Cottonwood. Drivers could catch I-17, go to Phoenix, and from there catch I-10 and go to Los Angeles. All the other roads in all of Arizona were closed and my road was open. I drove a big plow truck. I worked straight nights at Oak Creek Canyon. It rained there all the time, so there were rockslides. Somebody needed to monitor those roads all night. I liked working as a night shift lead man. I was always out.

They had different jobs for me. When it was raining hard, I was on rock patrol. We had slides that pushed rocks onto the road. I'd plow them off to keep the road passable. Then they had what they called *star watch*. I would drive up and down the roads in my pickup and watch the stars. As soon as I couldn't see anymore, I radioed the crews because it would start snowing within a half-hour. Usually, no stars meant a big storm was coming in from California. Then we had a storm patrol. A storm may start and end, but if forecasters predicted more bad weather, I stayed out in the truck all night. I watched for the next round of snow, and at the first sign, called out all the other crews from the other camps.

There were about six camps up there, and we all had to be on the radio. My radio reached to Phoenix. The governor would listen, too. When necessary, I called the different foremen of the different yards and said something like, "I'm over here on 89 with a lot of folks stuck inside, and it's starting to snow good, so you better get your trucks moving."

The first winter I lived in Flagstaff we had 265 inches of snow. It was crazy. That's over twenty feet of snow, and it never melted because we were hit by one storm after the other. The roads were closed to the point that the government had to fly in supplies to the Navaho reservation because they were totally cut off. The state brought in huge snow blowers and basically narrowed I-40 and I-17 to one lane and piled the snow up on either side of each. It was like somebody took a giant knife and sliced the snow off the road. They salted and dried it, but sometimes traffic was still limited to emergency vehicles only. There was a place out there called Mormon Lake Lodge that was built in 1924. Mormon Lake is the largest natural lake in Arizona. It's a big pond, really. It's not all that deep, but every winter they had the national dog sled races there. The races were televised and the lodge filled up. Once, during that crazy snow, the lodge was closed. Lil and I went out there to look at the deep snow in front of the lodge. It's a two-story building, and you actually go up the first story to get on the proper first floor. The snow was up to that second-floor balcony. You could step off the balcony and stand in the snow. That's how deep it was. At one point, we got stuck in our cabin because the snow was over the roof. I had the firewood stacked against the outside wall right under a window. I opened the window, dug the snow out of the way, and grabbed firewood to bring it in. Our only heat was the wood stove. There was snow almost year-round that year. Even in June, July, and August, when it got hot, the mountain peaks, which are 12,000 feet high on the north side, had snow. Lil and I had the ski boat and kept it parked outside the cabin we were living in. Well, we didn't see the ski boat until spring.

DAN

I HAD SOME WILD FRIENDS. I met Dirty Dan when I was still working for the state. He transferred from the main yard over to Oak Creek Canyon. I'll never forget one time when he was running a loader. When driving a loader, you have to keep your bucket down about a foot off the ground, and you have to watch it because roads are uneven, and the loader will bounce. Dirty Dan was going over a cattle guard and I was following him. I tried to yell at him, "Raise your bucket up!" but it was too late. He hooked the cattle guard. It stopped the motor and he went forward hard. His face cracked the windshield, and it was a perfect imprint of his face the glass. I couldn't help but laugh. We had to fill out an accident report. We were laughing so hard it took us two hours. After that, the state put shoulder harnesses in the cabs.

Dirty Dan was crazy in a lot of ways. He was a gangster. He was an armed burglar. He was a motorcycle gang member. He was Mexican and under the Mexican Mafia's control. He was also married. At one point he was in San Quentin in California, and the Mafia ordered him to kill a guy in prison there with him. Someone gave him a shiv, which is a homemade knife you can make out of different materials. Dan made sure he was right behind the target in the chow line. As they were walking into the chow hole, Dan knifed the guy in the back. The guards carried loaded weapons and of course started shooting. Everybody else cleared out of the way. The problem was that the officers had only birdshot for ammo. They filled Dan up with birdshot. Dan claimed that the guy attacked him and someone else stuck the shiv in his hand. He said he stabbed in self-defense. No charges were pressed against him.

He was on parole and the state hired him. Arizona was an equal opportunity employer and because he was Mexican, they didn't want to make any waves, so they hired him. One time when he got in trouble with the law, he went up in front of the judge and the judge said, "Well, Dan I can put you away right now for ten years. But, I'm going to make you an offer, and I don't do this very often, so you better think about this. You can marry your girlfriend and make an honest woman out of her, and I'll suspend the sentence, or you can go back to San Quentin for ten years without parole." Anita already had two babies by Dan, and they lived together.

He looked over at Anita. Anita was saying, "Yes, yes, yes."

Dan talked with her, and he said, "Well, you know I'm going to mess around on you. I'm telling you straight up how I am."

She had it in her mind that she could change him. There was no changing Dan. They got married, but he had girlfriends. He liked young girls seventeen or eighteen years old. He had one for every day of the week except for two nights. One of the two nights was Anita's night, so he'd be with her. The other night was the night he had to rest. Otherwise, he introduced the girls by days of the week. He said, "Bob, this is Monday, this is Sunday, this is Wednesday," and so on. Anita was Thursday.

He got busted at work. He left his section of road, went into town, and picked up one of his girlfriends. I think it was Monday. He picked her up that night and figured she could make a few runs with him, and then he'd pull over to the side of the road and they'd get in the sleeper in the truck and take care of business. But, just as he was turning around, he smacked into a car that was on blocks. It was an old junk car, so Dirty Dan decided to take off because he wasn't where he was supposed to be. The guard at the club where he was came running out had memorized Dan's license plate number. According to that guy, the car Dan hit was brand new. Dan said it was about twenty years old. Either way, the state bought the owner a brand new car and fired Dan. Dan got rid of the girl before police got to him because he didn't want them to catch him with an unauthorized passenger in the state truck, but they arrested him for leaving the scene of an accident.

Dan was a typical Mexican looking guy—short, muscular, and well buffed out. He was a scrapper from the word *go*. He wasn't afraid of anything. I remember one night I had some stuff coming down on me and he called me up and said, "Why don't you come on over?"

I said, "Well, I've kind of got a party of my own going on."

He said, "Well, what's up?"

I said, "I got a call from Phoenix warning me that there's a guy all drunk and trash-talking my name. He says he's got some buddies with him, and they're coming up to pay me a visit. I'm going to wait for them here."

He said, "Really? You got a call from Phoenix?"

I said, "Yes, I got a call from the Dirty Dozen warning me about it."

Next thing you know, I hear a motorcycle pull up, and it's Dan. He parked his motorcycle in the back of my house where people couldn't see it. He came in with a couple of guns of his own. I had fifteen or sixteen kinds of weapons.

Funny thing is Lil's boyfriend Larry was the one who was after me. He was a warlord and triple murderer, so it bugged him that I scared him that time when I went by the house and saw Lil there. Every time Larry got drunk, he talked trash that he was going to kill me. I had a feeling about it, so I never took the same road twice in a row. I always drove home from a different direction. One time I saw a guy, probably Larry, lying up in the mountains. I was on my way to work. I saw his rifle, but he wasn't able to get a shot off at me. I was right. I found out later it was him. I hunted him down and caught him in a bar. I just beat the snot out of him, broke his arm, and put the boots to him really hard. I said, "Next time you see me on the bike, and you've got a gun, you better shoot me because I will find out about it, and I'll be coming for you again." He backed off.

Larry went to prison for killing an elderly couple. Plus, he was a big time racist. As matter of fact, he had the Ku Klux Klan tattoo. When he went to prison, wardens put a big black guy in the cell with him. The guards probably figured the black guy would knock some sense into Larry. The next morning when the chow bell went off, Larry got in line and went for chow. The black guy stayed in bed. Finally, the black guy was supposed to be out of bed, and the bed was supposed to be made by eight o'clock. Guards went to the cell to wake the black guy, but he didn't wake up. His throat was cut from ear to ear. Larry had cut his throat. He was a Dirty Dozen biker.

Lil lived with him even after he killed those people. She met him when he was out on parole. He had his own business tow trucking. As a matter of fact I even worked for him sometimes, long before they started messing around. We went out to the reservations and did repos because the Indians were really bad about not paying for their cars. They came into town to car lots, and if the company refused to sell them a car, they screamed discrimination and threatened to take the dealership to court. The car companies got sick of paying court and lawyer fees, so they told the lot managers, "Yes, let the Indians come in, even if they don't have money to put down. You sell them the car. We'll repo it later." Some of the Indians bought cars and took them up to the reservations, then they never made payments. Nobody had jurisdiction to go up there and get the vehicles except for the United States Marshalls. They wouldn't bother to repo a car, so the dealerships hired us. They paid us $2,500 to go up and get a car. We'd figure out where the person lived. I was good at taking marks, and Larry was good at hot-wiring ignitions. We sneaked around two or three o'clock in the morning and either hot-wired the car or hooked up the chains, popped the door open, put the car in neutral, and loaded it up on the truck and took off. Usually, the minute we started to take off, lights came on in the house, and a guy came out with shotguns. The Indian almost always shot at us, so we had to fly. Larry drove while I shot back at the Indian. We turned the car in and got our $2,500. Soon, every car dealership around town was hiring us.

SUICIDE

LIL HURT ME BIG TIME. There were times throughout my life that I didn't want to live anymore, but especially after we broke up. One day, I got on my bike and took off down 89-A going into Oak Creek Canyon in Sedona. I came up on about a half-mile straightaway with a 90-degree turn to the right. A tight bank was on the left. It had no guardrail and the bank dropped about 2,000 feet straight down into the canyon. I figured, *I bet I could fly at least a mile down the canyon before I hit the ground.* I had the bike wide open and was doing over 130 miles an hour toward that drop-off. When I got about halfway down the straightaway my bike shut off for no reason. It just shut down. By the time I got to the bank, I had to put my feet down because the bike was going so slowly it was almost falling over. I parked the bike, sat down and thought about it, and said to myself, "There is no woman worth ruining a perfectly good Harley over." I got up, checked out the bike, and found nothing wrong with it. At the first kick, it fired up and I never had any more problems with it.

I designed all my bikes to start on the first kick because some of the things I did, I needed to do fast. I fine-tuned them and was always messing with the timing and the carburetors. My bikes could sit for a month but still fire up on the first kick. That one was an FLH Harley, a reconstruct rigid extended frame chopper. The handlebars were shoulder-height baby apes.

I built all my own bikes. Like I said, I would take unnecessary chances. I never had a speedometer on any bike I owned. I never knew exactly how fast I was going, but I kept up with or passed traffic. Once I got on the freeway and asked a brother to clock me. I said, "Follow me in your truck, so I can get an idea of how fast I'm going when I'm on the freeway."

He tried to keep up. By the time I got to the end of the on-ramp, I looked back, and he was gone. I was way up the road. He said when we met, "I was doing 90 on the on-ramp and you were just pulling away from me. You were doing 130, 140, easy."

I said, "Wow, I thought I was just keeping up with traffic."

I did crazy things. There would be two semis. I would think, *Lock and load*, and I'd shoot right down between them and pass them that way.

My brothers would tell me, "You're crazy man. You're going to get killed."

I always said, "If I do, it will be quick." I didn't care.

One time I was doing business at a bank and they bounced a check or messed up a deposit, which set off a whole string of them bouncing more checks. I never bounced checks. I've had my account at Mascoma Savings now for seventeen years, and I've never bounced a check. I always make sure I have money hidden in there that I don't even record. Anyway, way back then my bank bounced a check on Friday. I called the main headquarters Monday and asked, "Why did you bounce my check last Friday?"

They studied all the records but I could tell they couldn't figure it out. The guy said, "Because Sunday night you withdrew $20. That made you overdrawn."

I said, "Yes, but you bounced my check Friday, before Sunday night."

He said, "That's the way it is."

I got on my bike and I rode it right through the automatic door and into the bank lobby. I was mad. I told the manager, "You people are ripping me off." There was a line of people opening up new accounts, and I made a big scene. I said, "You're stealing from me. There was no reason for you to bounce that check, and you bounced it anyway."

Two people left the line, walked out, and said, "We're going somewhere else."

The branch manager called the police. The Flagstaff Police showed up. They said, "What's your bike doing here?"

I said, "I'm really upset. They're stealing my money from me, saying I bounced a check on Friday because supposedly I was overdrawn on Sunday night by $10." I had all the paperwork to prove it.

One officer, the sergeant, said he didn't understand the papers. He said, "But I tell you what. Get your bike out of here and take off, and I don't have to arrest you. Just take off." So I did. I took off.

I did outrageous stunts like that all the time. I've used up enough lives for several cats. I believe that all those times Jesus decided he was just not letting me die. He had things for me to do, and I don't think my work is done yet. That's why as I started sharing and writing down my story; all of a sudden, I got this overpowering urge to really push myself on the therapy. I need to get my strength back up so I can get out of the hospital and get back to work. I have a lot to make up for because back in the '80s, all hell broke loose. I became a serious outlaw biker and did a lot of bad, bad things. My gang broke the law. Many times we broke the law.

INVESTIGATED

LIL AND I MADE GOOD INVESTMENTS. We had lots of real estate and bank accounts, but we worked anyway because we were bored. She worked in a pharmacy. I worked for the road department. Then the IRS stepped in and they investigated us. Lil and I weren't even together at that point. We were divorced, but we shared a lot of assets. She had a tax accountant who had cheated some other clients. They found out and reported him, so the IRS seized his books. He split the country. Gary Daniels was his name. He went to Sweden or Switzerland, somewhere over there where he had hidden a lot of money. When the IRS looked into our files, they nailed us for about $200,000 in back taxes, but with the penalties (and back then they *really* raised the penalties up), it was over half a million dollars. We had to sell off our investments at a loss.

We used to buy second trust deeds, which are an excellent investment. For example. people took out second mortgages on their houses and generally, at that time, they were three-year loans. They made payments of one percent of what the loan was for three years, but at the end of three years, they had to come up with a balloon payment for the total of the loan. Banks might get six months into the loans and decide they needed their money, or the people would struggle to make the balloon payments. Lil and I would offer the creditors 50 cents on the dollar. They took us up on it. For example, if you had a loan for $10,000, six months in we'd give the bank $5,000 for it. At the end of three years, we'd get the $10,000 from you. Meanwhile, we collected interest every month. So, on that same $10,000 loan, we might get $100 a month for 30 months plus the $10,000 at the end and we only invested $5,000.

Lil was a real estate broker. She was smart and lucky. She entered pools and always won tickets and prizes. The first Thanksgiving in Flagstaff, she won six turkeys from different drawings.

After we paid the IRS that first big amount, they went back beyond seven years to nine years and came up with another $100,000 that we owed. When we added up all the penalties, it was almost $400,000 again. We had some CDs left, but not many. At one point we'd had about 60 CDs. We didn't really have to work because we were making $50 a month for one, $300 a month for another, and $100 for another, and so on. The IRS pretty much wiped out our investments and knocked us down.

METH

I ALWAYS FOUND WAYS TO MAKE MONEY. I was doing meth by then, and I liked it so much I learned how to make it. Eventually, I was selling everything I made to buyers in San Diego, and from there it was distributed all over the West Coast. I had somebody take it out of Phoenix. I brought it down and dropped it off. He carried it to San Diego. I got paid by the guy in San Diego. My stuff was so pure they could cut it three times. I would get $10,000, and he would cut it in half and make $10,000 profit. In San Diego they would cut it a third time and make big money. From there it went to the distributors.

I had a little-known formula. Making meth was problematic—not the cooking part but finding the ingredients. When I started, some of the ingredients I needed were hard to get, so I learned how to make those chemicals using stuff I *could* get. Methylamine is one example. You couldn't buy it anymore because the DEA (Drug Enforcement Administration) forced companies to ship it and store it in drums with pressure-activated sensors. The minute you popped the drum open, the sensors went off. The FDA (Food and Drug Administration) was monitoring them. They knew right where you were, and they could show up if they wanted to. They started off with 50-gallon drums, and they dropped it down to 30-gallon drums. Then sensors were installed in five-gallon drums. One chemical was something used to clean out swimming pools, another was formaldehyde, and then chloroform, which I could get in different places. I also used acids like sulfuric acid, formic acid, hydrochloric acid, and a couple of others, along with sodium metal. It's been so long I can't remember everything. I went to the swimming pool place to pick up the one thing and went to any drugstore to get formaldehyde. For chloroform, I had to find a feed store. I always had a cover story like, "My kid needs things for his science class dissecting a frog," or, "I have two pigs to slaughter and need a gallon of chloroform." For the sodium metal I went to supply houses. Once, I said, "I'm running a little mine up in the mountains and using a sluice, but it's leaking. I want to put two sheets of sheet metal together and let them fuse, so I need the sodium."

The guy there said, "All right, that's a good story." I had all different stories like that and all kinds of aliases. I didn't buy too often at pharmaceutical chemical supply houses, but I had some, about six, spread out over Phoenix.

I used the Leuckart reaction. I think it was the same process Hitler used. He thought it would make Jewish people sterile, so he gave it to them. Instead, they were all happy and painting their "dormitories" and stopped sleeping at night. He reevaluated and gave it to his stormtroopers. That's one reason they could act so ruthless and conquer nations so fast. They were all speeding and tweaking like maniacs. I got introduced to meth in New York and then in Massachusetts. We took Dexedrine diet pills and then speed. Meth back then was crude. In the '80s it got a lot better. That's when I started making it.

I had a cookbook with all the details. I made a few copies but guarded them. It's complicated to explain. There were twelve different formulas in my book, but the main one I used was the Leuckart reaction. If I remember right, first I had to make methylamine, which cooks don't need anymore. I used ammonium chloride and formaldehyde. I mixed the ingredients together, cooked it, and cut it with chloroform to make metha-formaldehyde. To keep it from turning to gas, I cut it with 40 percent water. We had to make prop (ephedrine), and that was hard because we couldn't easily get the acid we needed. I used sodium metal to produce ephedrine. Sodium metal is a soft metal that reacts violently with air and water. It's packed in oil. If you take a little piece out the size of a pea, put it on the bottom of an eight-foot piece of plywood, and then pour water on it, you'll get two distinct explosions. They use it with depth chargers.

I needed a lot of help and somebody to constantly watch the lab because we had to cook the meth at 100 degrees Celsius. I kept a thermometer in the mixture to make sure I heated it only three degrees at a time. Once the mixture started bubbling like beer in a glass, I knew I had the right reaction. Then I raised it to 135 degrees. After that, I cut it with acids. I used Red Devil lye and Drano to neutralize the acid.

I put the bath on a separator funnel after I turned it into methamphetamine hydrochloride. It was liquid, and I injected it with nitrogen gas to turn it solid. To make nitrogen I took a three-headed beaker and filled it up a third of the way with salt, put the separator funnel on it, and ran a hose up into the methamphetamine. I had a second separator funnel and filled it up first with pure sulfuric acid along with the salt. Then I dribbled formic acid. Each time the formic acid hit, it created nitrogen. That went into a beaker and formed crystals. Once it looked like oatmeal, I poured it into a separator funnel and created a vacuum line. I used ether to clean the meth. Benzene was used, too, but it makes the stuff oily and sticky. I liked it clean. I did that seven times and got the meth to look like a toilet bowl disc. I chopped that up and got about a quarter of a pound of 100 percent pure methamphetamine. If we put that on the street, people would die, so I cut it three or four more times. Even then, my stuff would get people speeding like they've never even done it before. The whole process to cook one batch took about 40 hours. That quarter pound, once cut into a pound, was worth about $10,000. I usually ran four or five batches at a time. I had a whole system with beakers and a laboratory. My supplies, not counting the chemicals, were worth over $1,000.

Man, I was busy. I made batches in a semi-trailer that we could seal up. We dug out big trenches in the desert near the compound, pulled the trailer into the hole, and ran vent pipes out of it and covered the rest up with dirt. After every batch, we moved the trailer to a new location to avoid being caught. Sooner or later, though, people smell the odor. A lot of natural order comes from cooking. We had to do a lot to cover our tracks, but the police didn't come anywhere near us.

I was doing really crazy things on that drug. My daredevil spirit caused trouble. Because I used it to make meth, I always had my hands on sodium metal, and once I had a whole kilo stick of it. Of course, I wanted to see what the stuff that size would do in water. Well, my stunt made national news.

I drove out to a private golf course in Phoenix. I took the sodium out of its container. The entire kilo was coated in oil. I walked across the bridge of a big pond. I threw the stick as far as I could and ran off the bridge. I watched as the sodium hit the water and sank for a couple of seconds. Then, I swear, the entire pond shot up about 30 feet in the air. I took off. I split!

So many people reported the explosion that the ATF (Alcohol, Tobacco, and Firearms) sent federal agents to investigate. They found a dead piranha in the water. Well, kids used to sneak over to that pond to go swimming at night. The ATF started checking out the area's ponds, and they found five other ponds that had piranhas. They didn't figure out who or what caused the explosion, but it was on the news with the headline, "Mysterious explosion in Phoenix reveals piranha in the water." I did a lot of crazy things like that. I loved explosives.

I also thought I was immortal and that no bullets could kill me. One night, I walked into my house, and there was a guy there. He had been sent over from San Diego because people were trying to find out where stuff was coming from and they wanted my formula, so they tracked me down. The guy was a hitman there to get my formula and shoot me. I walked in my door, and he was standing inside my living room. He pointed his gun at my forehead and cocked it. He smiled and said, "You know why I'm here?"

I said, "You're not getting my formula." I started laughing. I said "Think you're going to get a bullet in me? Go ahead, shoot. I'm going to take that gun away from you. I'm going to stick it up your butt until you bleed out, and before I fall down, man, you're going to cushion my fall. If you want to play, we'll play. We can walk into hell together."

This guy was staring in my eyes, and all of a sudden he backed off. He said, "Fuck. I've met some crazy people in my life, but you're the craziest. I can see it in your eyes you mean every word you're saying." He un-cocked the gun and said, "I'm going to put my gun away. I'm going to leave. I don't want no trouble with you at all."

I said, "Believe it because that's exactly what's going to happen." I was so high on methamphetamine I knew even if I got shot in the head I wouldn't die right away, that the speed would keep me pumping long enough to do what I had to do. I just didn't care.

I had that attitude, toward *anyone* who threatened me. I didn't care about myself at all, and I would take chances. My biker brothers would say, "Whoa, man. You should settle down. You need to calm down. Do you want to die?"

I would say, "I really don't care." I meant it. I know I'm dying now, and it doesn't faze me at all, but for different reasons. I never thought I'd live past 30, and most of the kids I grew up with and hung out with died young because of the drugs and the lifestyle we lived. My brother Saul is still alive and we're both amazed that we are survivors.

Once, I couldn't deal with the misery in my life anymore so I took a .357, cocked it, put it to my temple, and pulled the trigger. It misfired. It just clicked and nothing else. I cocked it again and pulled the trigger. That time, I pointed it at the ceiling. The bullet shot out of the barrel and blew a hole through the plaster. I set it down and said aloud, "Okay, somebody's telling me something here."

Back in those days, I drove my bike 130 miles an hour and faster all the time. Most of the brothers couldn't keep up with me. I'd just fly ahead and get about ten minutes ahead of them. Then I'd pull over and wait for them to come down the road. I got my bike chewed up so many times. They'd say, "Are you trying to kill yourself?" or "Trying to get to your funeral?"

I just told them, "I just like to ride fast." I did love riding it fast. The faster the better. A couple of times I got chased by the police, but instead of stopping, I just opened my bike up.

One time I was on my way home, and a highway patrolman started chasing me. There was a line of Winnebago campers in both the high-speed lane and the slow lane, so I just shot in between them and got home. I left the off ramp and pulled up in front of the house, parked my bike, went into the house, grabbed a beer, and sat down on my porch. Here he came, the patrolman. He looked up at me, slowed down, and wagged his finger at me. I found out he lived two streets over from me, so he recognized who I was. The next morning, I got on my bike and I went cruising over by his house. I put the clutch in and cracked it as loud as I could crack it. He came running out on his porch. I wagged my finger at him. I said, "I know where *you* live, too."

About half of the time I would outrun them and lose them, but they made up for it the times that they caught me. I remember one night I was cruising down to Phoenix. It was one of the first times I had put exhaust pipes on my bike. Usually, if I bought parts that had the pipes, I took an iron bar and busted them out because I liked my bike to be really loud. I was driving down one of the streets at about eleven o'clock at night, and this motorcycle cop was going the other way. He saw me and hit his lights. Then he turned around and started chasing me, so I took off. I flew down the road, thinking, *Well, that's fine. I'll shoot away and then I'll find a side street. I'll whip around that, and when I can't see him anymore, I'll pull up in a driveway and shut off my lights and wait until he goes by. Then I'll take off the other way.* I went up and down streets, but he stayed with me for a little while. Then I got into a place where I could really open it up. All of a sudden the squad cars were coming up the other way. They formed a roadblock and stopped me, so they caught me.

That guy was a big motorcycle cop. He was a lot bigger than I was. He came walking over and said, "Didn't you see me?"

I said, "Yeah, I didn't need to stop."

He asked, "Yes, well, how come you didn't stop when you saw me with my lights?"

I said, "Well, look what you're driving, and look what I'm driving. If my brothers saw me pulled over by a cop on a Yamaha, I'd get more crap from them than I'm going to get from you."

The sergeant started laughing about that. He said, "I see your point." His brother rode a motorcycle. One of the other cops started writing tickets for me for attempting to elude and all this other stuff.

Because I worked for the state in Flagstaff, I knew the places where all the highway patrolmen sat. If I knew there was one up ahead of me. I would take the exit before it and skip the spot. I studied all the highways, side roads, and different options, so I knew escape routes and hideouts. They came in handy.

I used a '67 Camaro to run drugs from underneath my house. Around two in the morning, I would do night drops, carrying the stuff in my Camaro and driving it to a drop down. The competition watched me sometimes. One night, they started following me. They wanted to find out where I was dropping. They were in a van. My Camaro was souped up to go fast. I played with those guys on my tail for a while. I slowed down and let them catch me, and then I sped up again. Over and over, I did that, hoping they'd get tired of playing. Finally, I got two miles ahead of them and pulled over on the shoulder of the road right up over a hill in the middle of a curb. I waited. A few minutes later, here came the van. There was a light on inside the back, and I saw two guys. One guy looked out the window and saw my Camaro parked as they passed me. I had my lights off, but he saw me. He yelled out, "There it is, there it is."

They hit the brakes, and I started up and pulled in behind him, following them down the hill. They pulled into a rest stop. I pulled right in with them. I got my pistol out, and I said, "Okay, we're all going to settle this once and for all." They stopped real quick and I started thinking, *Wait a minute, they might have a half a dozen guys in the van.* I just whipped around real quick and got back on the freeway. They started chasing me again. Then it got crazy. I was dodging them and going fast. I skirted them and when they jerked over to follow, my move caused them to roll the van over. The van flipped in the road, and the last time I saw them there was one guy lying out on the pavement. It looked like the other guy was hanging out the window and squashed by the van. I just kept going. When I got down to where my partners were, I told them, "I picked up a tail, so somebody's talking." We got real concerned and made a couple of phone calls to find out if it was the competition out of San Diego who had done it. If they had caught me they might have killed me. If not, they would have tortured me to find out my formula. Everybody wanted it, but I taught it to no one. I taught my two bodyguards because they helped me, but that was it.

Another time some low rider gang-bangers were cruising by my house. Half a dozen of them, Bloods or Crips, were in the car, and they had guns. They eased by a couple of times going real slow and staring, so I grabbed my machine gun. I always had two clips taped end to end. There were 28 rounds in a clip, but if I emptied one, I could snatch it out and stick it in the other way. Mark and load and I was ready. I got a beer, too, and sat down on the porch. Here they came again, and I started tracking them with the machine gun. Instantly, when they got right in front of the house, one of them saw the machine gun. He said something in Spanish to another guy. They all looked at my gun, straightened up in their seats, and took off. I heard one say, "Loco. Crazy." They didn't come back. I made a few calls and found out who had sent them. A contact through my gang had a talk with them. That took the heat off me for a while.

Eventually, I quit my job and made meth full time. Every now and then I'd pick up a part-time gig because I needed a front. Several other brothers had businesses, which meant we could easily launder money. One brother was part owner of a laundromat. A laundromat is one of the easiest places to launder money because you can literally wash it. The same goes for a dry cleaner shop. Plus, back then customers used cash for those services. If you walk around with a lot of cash and get picked up by the cops, they're going to want to know where the cash comes from. If the federal government gets involved, so does the IRS, so I had to be careful. Income tax evasion is a serious charge.

If you're making really big money, you *have* to wash it or you'll give yourself away. When they are suspicious, the first thing the police look at is your bank accounts. Then they watch your electric bill. I gave money to the people that would do the actual laundering. I paid them a percentage, and they reported the money on their taxes as income. I didn't give them all of it, just a chunk of what I grossed. Another good place was an arcade with pinball machines and games because there are really no records of what's coming in.

The bike club had good income from the meth, but there were so many hands digging into it, we really didn't clear all that much. So many people along the way had to be paid off. My connection down in Phoenix was paying off people in law enforcement. He got picked up one time at the airport. He had a bunch of cash, and he had a couple of pounds of stuff. The police arrested him, brought him in, and while they were booking him he made a phone call. He was in the cell for about two hours. Then police came down and gave him his briefcase with *everything* in it. They apologized to him and cut him loose. He had certain people on his payroll. He could make one phone call and get out of anything. I learned a long time ago there were people that would never get busted no matter what they did. They had the right connections and knew who took bribes. Nobody would ever touch them.

On top of cooking and selling, I used to go after big contracts, especially guys who had hurt little kids and women. I did some really bad things to men like that. To get paid, I took pictures when I was done with each job. Then, I met the people who hired me and gave them 30 seconds to look at the pictures. They paid me. I burned the pictures and crushed up the ashes.

I also did collections for organizations. Let's say somebody dealing for the organization ripped them off. The boss would tell me who to find and what the bounty was. My brothers and I would go out and get the crooks. We threw them into the back of our van, tied them up, and invited all the organizations who wanted the guy to come see. Then we auctioned him off to the highest bidder.

I worked and rode in Colorado, old Mexico, and Texas. I had some good pictures of us, our club, riding in a pack of 300. There were no colors shown in Flagstaff, but we were outlaws. Flagstaff was neutral territory. All the big clubs, the Hells Angels and the Outlaws and others, decided Flagstaff would be neutral territory. The Angels wanted it neutral territory because they had a farm outside of Flagstaff where they sent their people from California when they got too hot. They'd go out to that farm to cool off and maybe chill out there for a year or two. Police were after them and had warrants, so the Angels sent those guys toward Flagstaff, outside of Williams, Arizona.

Colors were displayed by patches. The clubs I knew were Hells Angels, Losers, Outlaws, Devils Disciples, and the Dirty Dozen. My club was called the Regulators. We didn't wear colors, but when bad guys ran into Flagstaff, we ran them out. We ran them to the New Mexico border or to the California border and told them, "Don't come back. If we see you back here again, you're going to disappear in the desert." There's a lot of desert out there.

I wore my leather jacket. I still have my leather. It's over 40 years old. I got that in the '70s. It fits me kind of loose now though because I've lost so much weight.

SECURITY

I GOT A NEW JOB. I worked security at concession stands in Phoenix. One guy had the contract from the state. He had stands at football games, basketball games, parades, the races, even the Grand Prix. Several of us brothers were bodyguards for him because the guy carried a satchel filled with about $250,000 in it all the time. We stuck to him like glue to make sure no one robbed him. He had 50 or 60 concession workers, so he made pickups from them. I got to see a lot of professional football and basketball games, the Grand Prix, and parades. We got paid cash under the table, so it was a good job. Any sporting event earned me $100-$200 just for being there with him for four hours. Back in the '80s that was a lot of money, so I was happy about it. The brothers told me I was psychotic, so I often had to go to Phoenix to play. That was fine by me because it was warmer down there. I rode my motorcycle year round and even though there was snow in Flagstaff, I took it real slow and careful to get off the mountain.

Flagstaff might be below zero, but when I got down to Phoenix during the day it was 60, 65, 70 degrees and T-shirt time. Phoenix is cool. In the early fall, it can get down to freezing, but not for very long. Farmers have orange and grapefruit orchards with heating pots between the rows of fruit to bring the temperatures up so that crops don't freeze. I thought grapefruits grew on a vine like cantaloupes. Once, I was looking at the trees down there, and I told people, "Those are big lemons."

A guy said, "You're kidding, right?"

I said, "No, those are the biggest lemons I've ever seen in my life"

He said, "They are grapefruits."

I said, "No way. Grapefruits don't grow on trees. They grow on vines on the ground. They're too big to grow on trees."

He laughed at me. He picked one and handed it to me. It blew me away.

He was brave for laughing at me. I was tough and not someone to laugh at. I was six feet, two and a half inches tall, weighed close to 280 pounds, and I was solid as a rock. I worked out with weights. I looked huge and strung out and my hair was wild. I was known by different names out west. People in Kingman gave me the handle "Shotgun" because I always had a sawed-off twelve-gauge with me. It was fourteen inches long from the tip of the barrel to the end of the handle. I wore it all the time in a holster that was wrapped around me. The shotgun was on my back underneath my leather jacket. It was easy to snap out. I used it many times. I was also known as "Mean and Ugly." When I ran collections, people called my partner and me "The Ugly Brothers." Of course, "Biker Bob" was a common one. "Big Bob" is the name that stuck.

I scared people, for sure. I pulled into a Circle K gas station store one night. It was winter, so I was wearing a ski mask and gauntlets. Plus, I was bulked up with a sweatshirt under my leather. I pulled into the station to put gas in my bike. I filled the tank up and walked into the store to pay. As soon as I did, the clerk raised his hands in the air. I thought he was being robbed, so I raised my hands in the air, too. We stood there and just stared at each other.

I said, "What's going on? Why do you have your hands in the air?"

He said, "Aren't you here to rob me?"

I said, "Here to rob you? Why would I be here to rob you? I just came in to pay for my gas."

He said, "You're riding a motorcycle, and you're wearing a ski mask."

It was funny, but it was scary because if he'd had a gun behind the counter and thought that I was a crook, he might have shot me. I kept my ski mask on, and I paid him for the gas. I didn't go back there again. I had lots of little experiences like that. Some are funny now when I think about them, but at the time they were not.

The brothers in Flagstaff and I really clicked. We biked all the time and did a lot of drugs together. We took care of some dirty business.

DEVIL

I ALWAYS CARRIED THAT SHOTGUN, BUT I DIDN'T ALWAYS SHOOT IT. Sometimes I showed it, and that made my point. Once, I had just gotten back to Flagstaff when I got a call. One of my partners Mark wanted me to come back down to Phoenix. There was trouble. We had a system; trouble could be a *disturbance* or a *war*. If a partner said *war*, I had a duffle bag loaded with everything: all kinds of guns, ammunition, hand grenades, and plastic explosives. For a *disturbance*, I took a small gym bag with a machine gun, a wooden hand grenade for an emergency, and lots of ammo. Mark said the deal in Phoenix was a war. I grabbed my duffle bag and biked on down.

When I connected with Mark, he introduced me to a young woman, and he told me she had gotten dangerously involved with some people who took her in. They welcomed her to stay with them because she was a single mom and broke, but the people turned out to be a witches' coven. The girl had two little boys. One was about one year old. The other was about two. The witches offered to buy the children off of her. She said, "Are you crazy? I'm not going to sell my kids!" She took off, but the coven started a campaign of terror. They followed her, broke into where she was staying, and she was terrified. They wanted to use her little boys as human sacrifices.

There were about 40 women in the coven, so the mom was desperate. Women in the group got pregnant on purpose. They kept the female babies and sacrificed the males through some kind of ritual.

I was already mad because I'd made two trips from Flagstaff to Phoenix and back in three days. That was a long ride on a motorcycle. Then, the story made me sick. We got into my brother Mark's van. I asked, "Where do these people live?"

She guided us to a nice house and said, "There it is. What are you going to do?"

I said, "Oh, I just want to introduce myself." I had my twelve-gauge sawed off shotgun in its sling. Plus I had a .357 and a .22 magnum along with knives. I kicked the door open. The thing that got me was that the room was painted red and black, and curtains were hanging everywhere. A bunch of witchy women in dark robes were inside. They were chanting. There was only one guy in the room. He had a tiny pencil mustache and a beard about a foot long. I walked up to him, figuring he was the high priest or something. I grabbed his beard and wrapped it around my hand. Then I shoved my shotgun down his mouth. I said, "You love Satan? You really love Satan?" This guy's eyes got really big, and he didn't know what to do. I said, "If you mess with this woman again, I'll be back, and I'll send you to Satan express. You understand?"

He whimpered, "Yes."

I took the shotgun out of his mouth. The women started getting really mouthy. I said, "If you mess with little children, you're all the same to me—garbage. You want to rumble? Let's go." I aimed the shotgun at the guy again, and they all reeled back. I used to get this really crazy look in my eyes, and they saw that look. I was so messed up on drugs, I would have shot them all. I wouldn't have cared. If you mess with little children like that, that's it. That's it.

I got back out into the van, and my partner said, "Man, you really are crazy, aren't you?" I told him the best way to deal with a situation like that is to tackle it head on. I learned that a long time ago. You tackle it head on, and you put an end to it. That scares the people you're dealing with because they are kind of insane. When they meet someone who's crazier than they are, someone like me with that wild look in his eyes, they know that one wrong move will get them dead. They back down real quickly.

I told the mom, "They shouldn't bother you again, but if they do, call me. I'll come right back down and deal with it." They didn't mess with that lady or her children anymore. I guess they went on to find somebody else who was weaker and didn't have people to help her.

Mark said over and over, "You really are crazy." That's what everyone kept telling me.

JUSTICE

I LIKED TO WORK CONTRACTS ON CHILD MOLESTERS AND WIFE BEATERS. An accusation could be a girlfriend or ex-wife trying to get even with somebody, so I always checked out the story to make sure what was actually going on and that the guy was truly guilty. I went after the worst ones and took care of them. Sometimes I didn't even charge for expenses.

This one friend of mine told me that her nine-year-old daughter was being molested by her ex-husband. Plus, he was going for full custody. He had the lawyers and the money to do it, too. He was in the movie business and worked on Hollywood sets. His company was making a movie down in Tucson. I checked her story out, and sure enough the story was true. I found out he would be a tough one to catch.

My brothers and I tried different methods to catch him. He had a clear road ahead of his rental house that took him to the highway on his way to work. We watched. He usually left about four o'clock in the morning. I bought a little air compressor at Home Depot. I tossed it onto the road to look like it had fallen out of somebody's truck or something. I figured he'd stop for it. My plan was to hide in the bushes and then jump him. But, he went right by it.

I knew a few professional dancers, also called exotic dancers. I always told people to keep their hands off them. They weren't prostitutes. My club owned a bar, so we had some dancers there now and then. One of our girls had gotten into a little trouble, so we stashed her over in New Mexico to cool off. I went to New Mexico and asked her to help me. I told her to wear a micro-mini skirt with no underwear and a fishnet top with no bra. Really early in the morning, we moved a car to the side of the guy's road. We popped the hood and had the girl stand in front of it. We hid the van off the road. I knew he would stop for her. About four o'clock, we saw the molester's headlights.

My brother Mike had given me a new zap gun. It shot 100,000 volts. He said, "You've got to try this." It had a belt hook so I hooked it on me. Sure enough, the guy spotted the girl and hit the brakes. He got out and ran over to her. Immediately, he tried to look up her dress. I went to grab the zap gun off my belt and I couldn't get it off. I zapped myself in the leg. That just made me madder. I broke the gun and threw it out in the desert. I grabbed my baseball bat. I ran to the guy and worked him over. Then I threw him into the van. We took him to a bar in town that we hung out at and really worked him over some more. Bad. I had some tent spikes that were as big around as my finger and had plastic spreaders on the end that kept them in place. I put the molester on his knees. I drove those spikes through both of his knees. I nailed his knees to the pavement. When I hit each one the last time, the bone closed up over the spike. He went out like a light.

My partner and I sat across the street in a shopping mall parking lot right where we could see and know. Soon, somebody found him, and called the police and the ambulance. We were sitting there drinking beers, smoking joints, and doing lines. The EMTs went to pick him up, and they didn't realize his legs were nailed to the pavement. He was just coming around when they went to lift him. He let out a scream that I remember to this day. I started laughing. I thought it was funny.

I look back now and I wonder how I'm alive after doing stuff like that. I didn't care if I was dead or alive. Nothing bothered me.

BIKERS

I CARED ABOUT MY GANG. I helped run it. There were six to eight of us who were on the council, and we had about 30 associates. The council was important. Let's say somebody was ripping people off and we found out about it. We had a council meeting to decide what to do with the crook. We picked up a guy once who was literally living in the gutters. We got him cleaned up, gave him a job, and gave him a place to live. He helped manage a bar the gang owned. The whole time he worked there money kept disappearing, and he kept blaming waitresses. We fired a lot of waitresses because of him. Then it turned out he was the one stealing the cash. So, we had a council meeting right there in the bar. We paid for all the customers' meals and drinks and kicked them out. We busted into the guy's room and found all kinds of loot: a big jug for the football pool, which had disappeared, a hand-me-down leather jacket one of the brothers had "lost," and cash. The only thing the guy said was, "I stuck around too long."

I said, "Yes, and you shouldn't have stolen from us." I wanted to shoot him, but the council decided we should just run him out of Arizona. I said, "All you're doing is sending him somewhere else to do the same bad stuff. A dog like that's not going to change. We ought to take him out in the desert and bury him." There were two votes with me and five votes against me. We did take him out in the desert and scare the heck out of him. We threw him in a car and drove him to our target range. We said, "You stand right here." We tied him up to a post. Then we got our guns out and shot targets all around him. This guy literally wet his pants. Then we untied him.

I told him, "You get your stuff. We'll drive you to the edge of Arizona. Don't come back. If we see you back here again, you're dead. We'll kill you." We rehired all the waitresses and apologized to them.

My motorcycle gang owned the bar, its restaurant, and a 40-acre compound right against the Navajo reservation. We were making a lot of money and had to invest and launder it different ways. The compound was something. It was east of Flagstaff near San Francisco Peaks—an active volcano. My brother Jimmy was the best Harley mechanic I've ever known in my life. He was out at the compound and started digging a swimming pool. When he dug into the earth, he discovered Indian ruins. At the time about half a dozen people were staying out there, and they all got into the search.

We had the whole property fenced off so there were only certain ways you could come in. We had an old cannon, a six-pounder, and I swear we had more guns than the military. You name it, we had it.

There were cribs set up so brothers could crash there. Sometimes we needed to get out of town and cool off. It was so close to Navajo land that the police wouldn't try to get on it. Federal agents might try. We had a couple of Navajos in our club, which gave us extra protection. A lot of people disappeared on their reservation, especially undercover agents, FBI agents. There was also a lot of Satanic worship out in that geography, and the Satanists killed people for human sacrifices.

In town one time we had a going away party for a brother who was moving up to North Dakota. There were about 250 motorcycles in his backyard. We roasted a side of beef, and we had a row of 5,000 firecrackers. When we set them off it sounded like a war was going on. His neighbors called the police. About a half-hour afterwards, as far as I could see, there were sheriff cars, state police, city police, and unmarked cars stacked up and down the road. A whole bunch of cops stood around wearing bullet-proof vests.

Finally, they sent this one old sergeant up there that everybody knew. He said, "We got a report of automatic weapons being fired."

We started laughing. The paper from firecrackers was ankle deep on the ground. I said, "No, we set off a row of firecrackers. There are still some lying around here."

He saw them and said, "Okay."

Everybody was packing weapons. I'm sure he was relieved because those cops knew that if they came in there it was going to be bloody. A lot of guys in the club would rather get shot than behave. We just assumed that if cops were going to hassle us, we'd hassle them right back. We had our own vests, and most of us loaded up our weapons with silver-tip ammunition that could go through three vests in a row. I know.

We tested it. We put three vests together and shot with a nine-millimeter silver-tip. It went through all three vests. That will bring down anybody.

We had a car hood about a mile away out in the desert and we put our targets on it. We drew them on with spray paint. We shot from a mile away with automatic weapons. Sometimes the police flew over in helicopters. I could spot them looking down on us with their binoculars. I bet they were saying, "Man, these guys are sharpshooters. If we raid, a lot of people will get hurt." They knew we had guys there all the time who weren't afraid to rumble. We always had a minimum of six guys on the compound, but sometimes there were 40 or 50 of us.

Another time we got some attention when we took a case of dynamite up to the Grand Canyon to Lake Mead. It was the Fourth of July. About 30 of us bikers, our old ladies, and our kids were up there with half a dozen boats. We camped way out in the middle of nowhere. We set off six sticks in the water and all it did was go "poof" and make little bit of bubbles come up. I said, "That's no fun." We took the whole rest of the case, that's 138 sticks of dynamite, and set it on top of a sand dune. We rigged a detonator to it, with the caps in one stick and the wires running down. We ran that wire 200 yards. My buddy and I got behind a huge log. One end was burning and I had a side of beef cooking on it. There were people shooting off fireworks all up and down the lake. Well, we lit ours, and all anyone heard was "KABOOM!" It echoed off the canyon, all the way up the Grand Canyon, and all the way back down it for about fifteen minutes. Boom, boom, boom, boom, boom . . . . Then it got real quiet. We heard no more fireworks after that.

Later, everyone went to sleep, but I stayed up until about four o'clock in the morning. About five o'clock, it was just getting a little light out, and I woke up hearing motors. It was the Coast Guard, fish and game agents, the park service guys, and the sheriff's department on a bunch of boats. They didn't come in very close. They yelled at me, "Did you guys hear an explosion last night?"

I yelled back, "Yes, I did, a real loud boom."

"You know where it came from?"

I pointed different directions and said, "Over there and then over there and over there and over there."

One asked, "You don't know anything about it?"

I said, "No, of course not."

About that time the brothers marched up where I was. They had AK-47s and M16s and stuff, and the police just looked at that. Their eyes got real big and bright. They said, "You guys have a good time," and they took off. They didn't bother us again, but that would have been another bloody one, and we would have won that one because we had cover. They were in boats. We would have wiped them out.

I was a violent individual. Now, I'm older and people see me in passing, like here at the hospital, and say, "Bob, you're so nice." Meanwhile, I'm thinking, *No. You've got no idea who you're talking to. If you knew me* . . . . They have no clue about my history. Sometimes I say, "If you knew me twenty years ago, you wouldn't think I was so nice."

One of the things I used to do for the club was find some redneck bar, park my bike out where my brothers could see it, and go in and get everybody in the bar mad at me. The trick was to buy one beer and nurse it while everyone else got wasted. I sat with my back to the wall at first and watched for a while to spot the bully. There's always a bully. He taunts people around the room while you act all weak. Finally, it's your turn. Well, when a bully started pushing me around, my whole attitude changed. Grown guys have said to me right then, "I think I've made a mistake."

I'd say, "Yes. I'm it." I'd get them so mad they wanted to kill me. I would tear them apart. I would give them back everything I'd seen them give to other people, plus interest. At first people cheered me on, but eventually I'd hear them yell, "Stop! You're killing him!" Well, the whole idea was to give those bullies beatings they'd remember the rest of their lives so hopefully they would change. About the time I started swinging, the club would pull in and we would all rumble. That was entertainment, literally, for my brothers and me. Sometimes, though, the club would roll on by and leave me hanging! That's why mine was a one-kick bike. My gang was violent, but we still lived by a code. We did a lot of stuff, a lot of stuff I will never tell anyone.

Most of my guts actually came from the methamphetamine. I've always been a fighter, thanks to my mom, I guess, but meth made me crazy. I used to do lines all day and all night. I'd stay up for four or five nights in a row, until I started hallucinating. Then I took a Valium or two. The Valium put me down for six to eight hours. Then I got up and started again. I never snorted or shot up the crystal meth. I used to eat it. It's got a nasty, nasty taste, like if you stick your finger in your ear and lick your finger. I wrapped the powder up in a tissue and ate it because I didn't want to ruin my nostrils, and I refused to shoot up. After the heroin, morphine, Dilaudid, Podiapn, and Demerol in the '60s, I vowed I'd never put a needle in my skin, which is why I hate to do insulin every day now.

I did a lot of crystal meth, though, for a long time. I always packed an eight ball with me. It's an eighth of an ounce, so about three and a half grams. It was $20 a gram. A gram would get me off four or five times. I cut it into lines and ate it. I did not eat much food. I mostly just drank coffee. Still, I was huge. I was intimidating on my bike.

GOOD

I WASN'T ALWAYS ABOUT BEING BAD. There were many things that my gang did, like the MDA (Muscular Dystrophy Association) run for Jerry Lewis's kids. I've always had a tender spot in my heart for kids. The MDA runs were cool. I used to have a great picture of us. Somebody got on a bridge over the highway and took a great shot of 300 bikers rolling down the road. We took up one whole lane. There were motorcycles as far as you could see.

I remember going on one particular MDA run when it was pouring rain. The rain started Friday and didn't stop the whole time of the ride on Sunday. We met at the Harley Davidson dealership in Flagstaff and partied down a little bit. The plan was to ride 100 miles then meet up at a brother's house, where we had a band set up for a huge party. I never had a front fender on my bike, so any water always squirted up and hit me right on the forehead. That day was nasty, but we made the run anyway. Well, the last leg to the brother's house was a dirt road about a half-mile long. It was pure mud. When I rode into the guy's yard, some other brothers stopped me. I was covered head to toe in mud. They said they had to hose me off to identify who I was. I didn't mind. Once they got the mud off my face, they said, "Okay. It's Big Bob."

Not having a front fender was strange to most people. Once, I had a girl riding on the back. It started raining, and I couldn't see, so I tilted my head to the right to get out of the water spray. She grabbed my ponytail and pulled me back over and held my head there. She said, "I'm getting water in the face!"

I said, "Hey, I'm the one driving!" It was funny.

Another time, a big wasp got stuck between her and me and stung me on the back. I couldn't stand it. Wasps aren't like bees. Their stingers stay in, and they keep stinging you. I kept telling her, "Get that wasp off of me!"

She was going, "Shoo, shoo, shoo." I had to pull over and get it off because it stung me about fifteen times.

148

I wasn't afraid of weather or getting dirty. The gang had a shop, which was kind of like our second clubhouse. A brother named Fred lived up the street. He wanted someone to sandblast his bike frame so he could paint it. He asked me, "What will you charge?"

I said, "Twenty bucks an hour, but I want to shower at your house when I'm done because there's no hot water at the shop." Fred said that was not a problem. He headed on down to the shop while I worked. I used his garage to sandblast the bike. I came out and I was covered in laser grit. My shirt, my jeans, my beard, and my shoes were coated. It was thick. I went up to his house, showered, and put on clean clothes. It had started snowing and was freezing cold outside. The visibility was terrible, so I called down to the shop and told the guys that if I wasn't there in fifteen minutes, come look for me on the road. I got on my bike with my hair and beard still wet. I flew down to the shop. I walked in to see everyone partying down, drinking and eating with the music up. Brothers and sisters were everywhere. When I walked in, all of a sudden, they got quiet. Everybody stared at me. Fred had a camera and got right up in my face and took a picture of me. I said, "What's going on? Is my zipper open or something?"

He said, "No, man. Go look at yourself in the mirror."

My hair was down, and it had frozen during my ride. It was straight back and up in the air. My beard was pushed out and frozen on either side of my face. There were icicles running from the ends of my mustache all down through my beard and sticking out about six inches on either side on my face. They blew the picture up to poster size and made me the poster child for the month.

We did some good deeds and had fun, but we were bad. We were with not with the AMA, the American Motorcycle Association. We were one-percenters. My gang was outside. I don't conform. I've been a non-conformist most of my life, so it's only natural that I'd be a one-percenter. I loved the lifestyle. One of the things I really loved was flying down the road at well over 100 miles an hour. There's a sense of freedom—like you don't answer to anybody—and you live life the way you want. I did a lot of runs with those brothers. A million miles.

RHONDA

I MET RHONDA WHEN I WAS HEAVY INTO METH. I worked the night shift plowing roads. I worked on the roads straight nights from six to six and cooked meth all day. Rhonda was a waitress at Denny's. I stopped in there at three every morning and had coffee. She kept bugging this buddy of mine. He worked on my shift, and his girlfriend worked with Rhonda. He told me, "Hey man, you're in trouble."

I said, "Why?"

He said, "Because Rhonda wants to go out with you. She's bugging my girlfriend and me about it. Just go out with her one time."

I didn't want to date her at first. I told him, "She's too young. She's way too young."

He said, "No. She goes out with guys your age."

I was in my middle forties. Finally, I gave in. I figured, well, the first two women were older, so maybe a younger one will be better. The next thing I know we are living together in my house. One morning I casually said, "One of these days maybe we'll talk about getting married." That was the wrong thing to say. The next thing I knew, she had picked a date and was sending out invitations telling everybody we were getting married. I didn't ask her or give her a ring. I just mentioned it. She was nineteen. I had to make her a phony ID so we could get into bars.

Because of the drugs and lifestyle, most of the time we were married, those memories, are blurry in my mind. We dated less than a year, and we got married down in Clover Creek Canyon in Arizona by a justice of the peace. I didn't want to get married. At the wedding I said to a friend, "I don't think I should be doing this."

He said, "It's not too late, man."

It was hard for me to love again and let go like that because Lil had hurt me so much. I was lonely. I went ahead with it. We actually had two kids.

I liked her family and met some cool people through Rhonda. Her step-father Papa Mike had cancer. His cancer went into remission, but Papa Mike got really down and was getting lost a lot. He couldn't function too well. We figured it was just post-cancer depression, but later doctors discovered that the chemo had given him some kind of palsy. Rhonda's uncle Big John was huge. He was six-foot-eight and probably weighed over 300 pounds. He and I decided to cheer up Papa Mike. We found a limited edition Sportster that Papa Mike could ride. The seller wanted $4,000, but when I told him who it was for, he dropped the price down to $2,500. Big John and I went in on halves to buy it. We got Papa Mike to come over one Sunday morning. We brought out the bike and said, "Mike, this is for you."

He flipped out. He said, "You guys are crazy! You guys are crazy!"

I said, "Nah. This motorcycle is for you. You need to ride, man."

Papa Mike's friend Brian was there, too. He and I just clicked. We took Papa Mike on five runs together. Brian was very protective of Papa Mike. The disease got to the point that Papa Mike couldn't ride anymore. He was in the passing lane doing about 40 miles an hour with a whole lot of trucks and cars stuck behind him. We got him to pull over, and that was it. His disease, by then, was like Alzheimer's or dementia. I was over at his house visiting once, and he went into the bathroom and was there a while. Then I heard him yell, "Help! Somebody help me!"

I ran in there and opened the door up. "What's the matter?" I asked.

He said, "I don't know how to get out of here."

That's when we all realized we had a big problem. He didn't last very long after that. Crazy Brian and I really missed Papa Mike. We were tight from then on. We rode together and did some wild things. For example, a brother was getting married and Brian said, "Bob and I will provide the meat for the wedding. We'll kill an elk."

I said, "Man, let's not give him meat as a gift." I went along with it, though.

Well, early one morning we rode out to find a range cow. I told Brian we couldn't kill anything with a brand on it. There are still a lot of wild cows in Arizona. Sure enough, we spotted one that wasn't branded. I ran down along side of it and had a .22 magnum pistol. I shot that cow six times and it did not drop. I had to reload. Brian and I lost sight of the animal. We found it, and I followed it for about a mile. Finally, I shot it right behind the ear and it dropped. Someone had to go back for the truck, so I started walking back. I had a .357 magnum in the truck. I finally got to the truck and shot the .357 in the air to signal that I was at the truck and was about to drive to where Brian and the elk were. Well, Brian came running full speed at me and said, "I have a backhoe. We can use that. We should have brought shovels with us!"

I said, "What are you talking about?"

He said, "Didn't you shoot him?"

I asked, "Shoot who?"

Brian said, "This guy came riding out of the woods on horseback. He was a range protector, and he rode straight toward you. You didn't see him?"

I said, "No, but if I had seen him, I probably would have shot him."

He said, "Oh, man, I thought you did shoot him. I thought we were going to have to bury him and his horse."

He was totally levelheaded and trying to figure out a way to dispose of a body and evidence. I thought that was cool. That impressed me. Brian had a lot of backbone. He didn't panic. He always put business first. We were good brothers. Like blood.

CRACK

MY INSTINCTS WERE RIGHT. I made a mistake marrying Rhonda. The biggest mistake of my life. She turned out to be a crack whore. In time, she would sell her body to anyone who would give her a line. It got bad. Every morning, I changed the kids' diapers before I left to go cook. I changed them, fed them, and put them back in their beds. Well, one day I came home around four in the afternoon. As soon as I turned my bike into the driveway, I heard a baby crying in the house. My little girl was standing in the crib. The diaper I'd put on her in the morning was down around her knees. She was covered in crap. My little boy had fallen out of the bed and had a big knot on his head. He also had a dirty diaper. I went in my bedroom and found Rhonda spread eagle on the bed, naked, out like a light. I grabbed the kids, tossed all their clothes and diapers, took them down the hall and put them in the bathtub. I got them all cleaned up and fed them. Then, I went up and grabbed Rhonda by the hair. I dragged her down the stairs, took her out the front door stark naked, and threw her off the porch. I tossed her car keys and her purse onto the ground and said, "You hit the road. You go check into rehab and when you get your priorities straight, you come back and we'll talk. These kids are number one." Their names were Rachel and Zachary.

I was tired of living so hard. I was planning one last batch that would kind of free me, financially. I was going to completely retire from cooking. I had found a boat in San Diego that I wanted, an 80-foot boat. It had GPS, radar, and ship-to-shore radio. The seller wanted $80,000. Crazy Brian, his wife, Rhonda, and I were going to buy the boat and then sail it to Hawaii. In Hawaii, we would mail in our citizenship papers renouncing our American citizenship then head down to the Solomon Islands. We would live out our days in the Solomon islands. They're about 1,500 miles northeast of Australia. Of the 2,500 islands down there, 1,500 have freshwater, but only 600 have people on them. You don't have to have neighbors. You can make runs to Australia for food and supplies, but we could grow most of our own food. That was my plan. I did a lot of research.

When Rhonda got detoxed, she came back to talk. I told her, "Okay, if you want to get back together, this is the way it's going to be: no more drugs for you at all." I was cooking and doing meth, but I had an unbelievable ability to control it. It helped me get through those night shifts. I put the word out about Rhonda, and everybody respected it. I was a crazy guy, and everybody was scared of me. I told them if they so much as gave Rhonda an empty wrapper, I would come after them. She figured out that the only way she was going to be able to get drugs again would be if I was dead or in prison. So, she turned me in. She called the police on me. Rhonda told them about the meth, and she told them I had five million dollars in a strongbox buried in the backyard.

I was in my house and heard car doors closing. I looked out the window and saw cops putting their vests on. I grabbed my machine gun and slapped a clip filled with silvertips into it. I went into the living room and saw two of the cops standing at the back door. Three were at the front door. I thought, *I'm going to fire a quick burst at the front door then empty the rest of the clip from here, get onto my bike, and take off.*

I took aim. My little girl was sitting right there. She said, "Are you going to shoot somebody, Daddy?" She wasn't afraid. I always took the kids target shooting with me. The reality hit me. I thought, *This is a wooden house. If I start shooting, the cops will shoot, and they'll hit the kids.*

I wasn't afraid. I was ready to shoot until she snapped me into reality. Before that, I was thinking, *Here we go. Party time.* But when Rachel said that, I put the gun down. When the cops searched me, the chemicals I had weren't enough to make anything, but they had an FDA agent with them. He took one look at the chemicals, winked at me, and said, "Leuckart reaction, huh?" Then came the ATF, the DEA, and the IRS because Rhonda had told them I had five million dollars buried.

I told the agents, "Well, tell you what. Just give me ten percent of that five million, and I'll give you the rest. You won't find it."

He said, "Oh, we'll find it."

154

When I got busted, I was worried. So was my lawyer, but the DA on my case said that if I came up with $100,000 the charges would be dropped. The feds heard about that and put a lock on any deals. They said they would seize anything I had, even bail money. They searched my property with metal detectors. They found something, all right. I had a piece of my rib and two nerve ganglions that the doctors had removed. They were stored in an Arnold pickled pigs' feet jar filled with formaldehyde.

Funny story. Once, Dirty Dan was over and really drunk. He saw that and said, "Hey man, I'm going to eat this pickled pig foot."

I said, "Dan, you are welcome to it, but it's not a pickled pig foot. It's my rib." He dropped it back in the jar and scrubbed his hands raw.

When the police found that rib, they called me down to the DA's office. He said, "Among other things in your house, we found a human rib and other body parts that look like they came from a spine. What were you doing with them?"

I said, "We had a barbecue and the person who ate that stuff won a prize."

He had no sense of humor. He tagged me with 50 counts on the drugs and weapons and added one count of cannibalism. The police also indicted me on doing burglaries in three different towns, at least 60 miles apart, at the same time on the same night. I asked my lawyer, "How come they are charging me with all this stuff?"

He said, "They're going to charge you with every unsolved crime because when they read the indictments in court, and the grand jury hears them, they're going to think something is big time wrong, and that will prejudice the jury and help the police."

I couldn't believe it. I could have actually paid the DA off with $100,000, but I didn't have the money. I knew people who got busted and got out of it. Once, the FBI was after Lil and Larry. He got busted again for something. I went over to help them get bail money together, and she said, "The FBI just pulled up out front. You need to hide in the closet. Don't let them know you are here." I didn't care if they knew I was there or not, but she made me get in the closet.

They talked to her and said, "If you can get Larry to do [this and this and this], all his charges will go away." I heard stuff that I will take to my grave with me. I knew then that if I talked, they would find out, monitor me, and later I'd have an "accident" and be dead. Any stories you've heard on TV about how crooked the government is . . . that's nothing compared to what I heard. I was shaking afterward. Larry, Lil, and I built a fire and wrote notes back and forth and burned every note. I will never repeat it. Larry did what they asked. I protected Lil. I guess it's weird that I still had a relationship with Lil and Larry, but she and I had business together even then, so I tried to keep things friendly. She came over to my place one night and wanted to sleep with me. I said, "No, Lil. I told you I don't play that game and now you want to cheat on *him* with *me*? No. I have no desire to be with you again. You betrayed my trust, and I never messed around on you."

As far as my indictment went, a payoff wasn't happening. The cops never found the five million in my yard. It wasn't there because it didn't exist.

JAIL

I AWAITED TRIAL AT FLAGSTAFF COUNTY JAIL. The bail was two million dollars. I couldn't come up with the cash myself because the law seized every penny I had and threatened to grab any money I used to try to pay a lawyer. So, I had to go with a public defender at the state's expense. I was there for 255 days and filed a motion for bail reduction. I got the hearing, and the judge knocked it down to $50,000. My brothers finally got with a bondsman and posted bail for me. I think the police would have kept me there for two years if I hadn't met bail. I mean, I was looking at 300 years of jail time.

When I was released on bail, I went straight to my house, but a state trooper and his wife were living there. The cops had seized my house and all my possessions. It really upset me because I walked in, and this guy was sitting on my couch with his feet up on my coffee table. He was watching my TV and eating out of my dishes. I kind of lost it. Well, not kind of. I grabbed him, picked him up, and threw him through the sheetrock in the living wall. I was going to kill him. It's probably good his wife was there. She was saying, "I'm going to call the police! I'm going to call the police!"

There was no phone in the house, so she would have to walk or drive about a mile down to a payphone. I said, "Go ahead, beat it." She thought better of it, so she didn't leave.

My brothers were with me. They grabbed me, and one said, "Man, you don't need this on top of everything else." I didn't care. I really didn't care. I was furious. The brothers calmed me down and we took everything. We even peeled the carpet up off the floor. We took the wood-stove. We took everything.

The trooper and his wife stayed there. I guess they put a sleeping bag down and slept on the floor. I had no place to live, so I stayed at the clubhouse. It was strange. I was financially and emotionally wiped out. Then I decided to run.

While I was in the county jail, Rhonda lost custody of the children because she got back into drugs. The cops busted her, and she was back in rehab. I got a camper, picked up my kids from where they were staying, and split toward old Mexico. A woman I knew was a border guard at night, and she let me slide through. I'm not sharing her name because I don't want her to get in trouble.

My plan was to make my way to Belize. Another brother of mine that I rode with had split Arizona and gone there because Belize has no extradition. All he had when he got down there was his motorcycle, the clothes on his back, a new ID, and a new passport. He ended up owning a big resort. He said I could work for him. He said, "You'll make good money, your kids will be taken care of, and you'll have bodyguards." Down there you could have somebody killed for 50 cents in American money. The economy was so poor.

I tried to hide. This lady I knew said I could come to bayou country in Louisiana. She said, "They'll never find you here." That was an option, but the kids and I stayed around the border.

Then, a brother in the club up in Flagstaff got into some real trouble. He got in way over his head, and I called in to check up. The council told me, "We need you up here to straighten it out. Nobody else can do it, and if you don't handle this, our brother will get killed."

The guard let me back across the border. I drove back up, took care of the situation, but was still broke, so I set up a meeting with an organization. I said I would teach their chemists how to cook my recipe. I asked for $250,000 and safe passage to Belize. They said they would arrange for payment at the final meeting. Rhonda somehow found out about it. I was at the last meeting about to wrap up the whole deal, and the next thing I know all these state troopers and unmarked cars show up. Guns were on me. I was looking at them and thinking, *Oh man, here we go.* That was it for me.

They searched my camper and found a sawed-off shotgun, so that was another charge they added to my tab. They found some needles in my camper, and I made them do a strip search of me right away because I don't use needles. The deputies checked me for tracks. I said, "The only reason needles are in my camper is because you put them in there." I was adamant about that. I did not want needles around my kids. That was another set of charges. I was looking at 75 years on the shotgun and

300 years on attempting to manufacture. We worked out a plea agreement, all totaled, for sixteen and a half years. I was in prison after that. I was supposed to stay in prison until 2015. The kids went to foster care.

Rhonda got a weekend pass from rehab one Friday and came to see me when I'd been in prison for about a week. I told her I wanted to see the kids. I would call her later, many, many times, and ask her to bring the kids. Every time, she'd say something like, "No, I'm busy," or she'd say, "Maybe Sunday." Then she got mean. I was on the phone with her once and asked her what she was doing. She said, "You want to know what I'm doing?"

I said, "Yeah, what are you doing that's got you so busy you can't bring my kids to see me?"

She said, "I've got a date with this guy and he's going to turn me onto crystal. Then I'm going to . . . ." She was very descriptive of what she was going to do for him. She was trying to drive me crazy.

She told the prosecutor a bunch of stuff and my lawyer said, "Yes. They know it's bogus. I'm not even going to tell you what it is. You don't need to be upset."

I got a hold of Crazy Brian. He told me he was in a bar and saw her dirty dancing with some guy. Brian punched the guy out and slapped her across the face a couple of times. Then he dragged her outside and said, "My brother's rotting down there in jail, and you're in here dirty dancing with this punk?"

It all made me sick. I found out the guy was called Davy. He was a hitman for one of the cartels in Columbia.

PRISON

I WENT TO ARIZONA STATE PRISON COMPLEX – DOUGLAS. It is six miles from the Mexican border. As a matter of fact, it is six miles from the exact spot where I crossed over into Mexico.

When I went to prison, nobody knew about that child molester I nailed to concrete. Police were investigating it but had no idea I was involved. At Douglas, this guy came up to me and said, "I understand you're the guy that nailed so-and-so to the pavement."

I said, "Where did you hear that?"

He said, "We have our ways."

I said, "Well, don't always believe everything you hear."

At least I had a tough reputation coming in, but I still had a lot to get used to. The dormitory didn't smell bad. It was big with fifteen or twenty pods and two people per pod. We had windows, too, without bars. At night it was quiet. I can't remember ever talking after lights went out. We had to be quiet because there were a lot of people in the dormitory area. If you made too much noise, you would easily get in trouble with the other prisoners. There were psychotic people around.

One guy got killed by his roommate over a postage stamp. These two cellmates were road hogs and actually real good partners. The one guy was writing a letter and didn't have a stamp. His cellmate's locker was open, he saw a stamp sitting there, so he took it. He figured his partner wouldn't mind if he borrowed a stamp because he could pay him back later when he got his commissary stuff. The next day, the cellmate was looking for a stamp because he'd written a letter, and he said, "Did you take my stamp?"

The other guy said, "Yeah, I borrowed it."

The cellmate said, "What do you mean you borrowed it?"

They got into a huge argument about that, and the cellmate pulled out a shank and stabbed the guy in the chest, the stomach, and plenty of times in other places. He killed him.

Each cell was in a pod. The cell was about four and one-half by five feet with a cement wall around it. It had two bunks and two lockers.

Then there was another one, another one, another one, all the way down the line. There were about 40 or 50 people per cell block, and there were four cell blocks per building, plus special private rooms for the trustees. The trustees mop and do janitor work. They are prisoners who get extra privileges for doing their work.

We woke up around six in the morning, and guards opened up the yard a little after that. One house at a time, we went to the chow hall to eat. It was open until eight o'clock at night. I always checked the day before to see what the menu was. If it sounded decent, like eggs, ham, or pancakes, I went. Most of the time it was disgusting.

After yard time, we went to classes or worked in the morning. Lockdown was at eleven o'clock in the morning. We had to return to our cells and be counted. They made sure everybody was there. Then one house at a time would go into lunch. We were out in the yard for the afternoon and then back at four o'clock for another count. This was a maximum security prison. Between four and five o'clock, we started, one house at a time, going to dinner. Usually, after that we could stay out until nine o'clock.

When we were free, we hung out at the track in the yard. The yard was mostly sandy with double fences around the perimeter. One job the trustees had was to rake the sand in the yard. When guards made patrols, they checked the sand for footprints going in the wrong directions. We had weight piles. We could play softball, baseball, horseshoes, and things like that. Most guys would lie on a blanket during the day or work out at the weight pile. Those were the two big activities. We all worked out. We needed to be tough in there because if you were weak you weren't going to last.

COMMISSARY

COMMISSARY WAS IMPORTANT. We got it every two weeks, but if you ran out of something, you could get it from another inmate because a lot of us had our own stores. We charged extra. For example, if you borrowed one pouch of tobacco, you paid back two. We did two for three with anything from cigarettes to canned food. When inmates finally got commissary, they paid you back. If they didn't pay you back, you didn't collect from the actual individual. You went to the leader of his race. The leader made sure you got paid back.

Everybody had the same budget to start with. There is no cash money in prison, but we got an allowance credit of twenty bucks a week. The commissary was basically a little store behind a window. It had tobacco, soaps, shampoo, deodorant, and things like that. You could also buy safety razors and all kinds of food like bread, peanut butter, jelly, milk, candy bars, chips, and all kinds of Little Debbies. There were guys literally addicted to Little Debbies. The boxes were 99 cents each, and guys would buy ten of them. For a while the prison had a snack bar where we could buy a hamburger, a burrito, or a milkshake. Every two weeks, I got to make a list, and that was my order form. I had to turn it in on Friday, and Tuesday my order was ready to pick up at the commissary. I just stood in line. When I got up there, I gave my name and then picked up whatever I had on the books.

People are surprised we could buy razors, but they were safety razors. We had to be clean shaven all the time, even mustaches. We could have a Hitler type of mustache but nothing could hang over your lips, and you could not have a full beard. The razors were worthless as weapons. It was much easier to take the lid off a can, find wood, or get a piece of fiber glass and make a shank out of it.

All prisoners could have a TV and radio but had to use headphones, and most had a few books. Everyone was allowed to keep a Styrofoam ice chest, which cost about four or five dollars at the commissary. Every day the guards passed out ice and sold soda pops. We needed that commissary because the cafeteria food was terrible. A lot of people didn't even eat in the cafeteria. They just bought food from the store and made their own lunches. Some had a little coffee pot they could cook in. The main lights were turned out after eleven o'clock, but you could stay up all night and read if you wanted to. You had a little lamp in your pod.

Prisoners read all the time. Douglas had a big library. We could go to the library to check out books, but most of us read from the huge law library. A couple of inmates were paralegals, and they helped others file appeals. They took online courses in prison and actually became paralegals while they were incarcerated. I filed motions and won all except one. I won the motion to see my kids early on. While I was in the county jail, I filed and lost the motion for a fast and speedy trial. The cops had violated my rights for that, so I filed a motion to have the charges dismissed. At that time, the district attorney had only 120 days after a person was arraigned to put him on trial, but I sat in that first jail for 255 days. The public defenders had slandered my character on a couple of the charges. Plus, every time I tried to file a motion for a speedy trial, my public defender said, "No, don't do that. I'm negotiating for an agreement." Well, I never heard from him. Then I was assigned a lady attorney. I immediately wanted to dismiss her and hire the best criminal lawyer in town, at the state's expense. I filed a motion that I could select my attorney and won the motion. The lawyer I wanted was too busy, but he had his partner represent me. A part of that guy's job was to have the lady public defender lawyer dismissed from my case. She was so embarrassed by the whole thing she never showed up in court.

Outside of that and once I was at Douglas, I represented myself. Once, a judge asked me, "Who prepared these motions?"

And I said, "I did all of it."

He said, "You did all of the research?"

I said, "Yes, sir."

He said, "I've got to tell you. These are some of the best motions I have ever seen in my life."

You need to show precedents when you file motions. The more precedents you show the better your chances are of winning. I overwhelmed him with the number I showed (28 cases on one charge). I quoted the decisions that came down on cases similar to mine. Word got out about my motions, so at one point I had a whole courtroom full of lawyers who wanted to see this criminal who filed great motions. Prosecution could argue against one or two cases. But 28? No.

The most important motion I won was to get a visit from my children. I argued to have a contact visit, and I won. When I got to see my kids, I was chained up, handcuffed to a chair, and armed guards stood over me. I saw my kids for ten minutes. That was the last time I saw Rachel and Zachary. Rhonda took them and disappeared. Maybe they went to Columbia. My outlaw biker brothers tried to find her. They wanted to hurt her, but I said, "No. When I get out, I'll deal with her." I had every intention of dealing with her. I planned to kill Rhonda.

RIOT

DURING MY FIRST FEW MONTHS AT DOUGLAS, I WAS SUCKED INTO A RIOT. I hadn't been there a month, and the whites and the blacks and the Hispanics decided to go on a food strike. The food was so bad I wouldn't even feed it to Black Cat. We went on a food strike, and that worried the prison administrators. Actually, it didn't worry them about the blacks and the Hispanics, but when the whites joined in, that's when they got scared. They brought in goon squads from the other eleven prison systems in the state.

No one could eat that food. It was disgusting. They served different things, but usually we had beans because we were only six miles from Mexico. Some Mexican outfit was coming in and cooking the food for us. There'd be pinto beans, but they'd be half-cooked. They'd give us a quarter of a piece of chicken. The drumstick was as big as my thumb. I don't believe it was chicken. I think they were cooking pigeons.

The night before the riot the warden came around and talked to us. He said, "Give us a chance. We've changed the menu, and we've got somebody else cooking the food now. Give us a chance tomorrow. Come to chow and see what it's like. We promise the food will be better from now on." The wardens went to all the dorms and talked to all the leaders of the whites and the blacks and the Hispanics.

During the night the blacks decided, "No, we're not going to chow." They sent word over to the whites, saying, "Nobody go to chow tomorrow in the morning."

The Aryan brotherhood ran the whites. The leader said, "First off, you guys don't tell us what we do. We tell you what to do. You don't tell us."

The blacks said, "If you go to chow, there's going to be a fight afterwards."

The Aryans said, "Fine, let it be a fight."

We went to chow, and I went over to this guy, an outlaw biker from California, named Kenny. *California Kenny* was his name, and we were the last ones out of the chow hall. We walked into the big square yard, which was about a half mile across. Everybody was gathered up into corners by race. Kenny and I were the last two to show up. It was quiet. That's what got me. The compound was totally quiet. We walked onto that scene, and Kenny said to me, "You know what this is going to be?"

I said, "It's going to be the Alamo all over again." There were about 130 of us whites and over 500 of the others. They had shanks, pipes, wooden clubs, and broken table legs. We were totally unarmed. When we got there the other races started coming toward us whites, and you could hear a pin drop. Nobody was saying anything. We approached each other, and when we hit, it was like a bomb went off. The fight was on, and we were really jamming. The whites were holding our own. I was on a flank. We couldn't let them get behind us because if they got behind us, they would've wound up killing us all.

The guards were up in the towers and on the roofs of all the pods. They had automatic weapons, but they opened fire with shotguns. Out of the corner of my eye I saw this club coming toward me, and I blocked it and nailed the guy who was holding it. I knocked him out.

It turned out he was the guy from the next pod in my dorm. It felt like bullets were flying right by me. I said, "That's it. I'm out of here. I'm going back to the dorm." I started walking back to the dorm and other guys did, too. They didn't want to get shot. Those guards had no problem shooting us.

Well, in came the goon squad in a straight line. I got about a halfway across the yard, and they made me lie on the ground. They took everything I had off of me. We sat out there from early morning until 11:30 that night in the hot Arizona sun. They brought porta-potties out. We had to sit cross legged with our hands on our heads all day. If you had to go to the bathroom, you raised a finger up, and they let you go to the porta-potty. Every couple of hours they gave us water.

Finally, the warden came and talked to us. He said, "Okay, here's the deal. We're going to let you go back into your dorms, but I want your word that you won't attack any of the guys that didn't participate in the riot." If there was a riot and all of your race was called out, but you didn't go, you were marked for death.

166

We gave our word to the guards, and they finally let us back into the dorm, but we were on lockdown for three months. That meant we were stuck in the dormitory for three months and only got out to go to chow.

GANGS

EVERY RACE HAD A GANG. The Aryan Brotherhood members were often kept in solitary confinement because they would kill their cellmates. They pretty much ran the prisons for the whites in America. My cell block was racially diverse, but in each pod we were segregated. Wardens try to never put a black guy and a white guy together or a Mexican and a black guy or a Mexican and a white guy. That would just cause trouble. In my time, and maybe it's different now, but I doubt it, when you were white, you hung out only with whites. If you were black, you stuck with blacks. If you were Mexican, you hung out with other Mexicans. If you got "out of race" you'd get killed real quick. If there was a riot, you stood with your race. If you didn't, once the war ended, you got a visit within 24 hours. A leader would say something like, "You're a white boy. You should've been out there with us, win, lose, or draw, and you weren't, so we're gonna deal with you." The Aryan Brotherhood is serious. For people who have never been to prison it sounds scary and crazy. It may sound unbelievable, but it's the truth and actually a lot worse than what people read.

Everybody new to prison got a *heart check*. Your race sent torpedoes in to rough you up just to see what you were going to do. Torpedoes are enforcers for the gangs. The Aryan Brotherhood sent two guys in on me, and I fought them. They went back to the Brotherhood and reported what happened. One of the leaders came over and talked to me and said, "Sorry we had to do that, but we had to see what your heart was."

I said, "Next time you do something like that, send men. Those guys were nothing."

He just looked at me funny and said, "You are all right."

I wasn't afraid. I was too stupid to be afraid of anything.

CULTURE

THERE ARE A LOT OF MISCONCEPTIONS ABOUT PRISON. Back then, there were more drugs in prison than there were on the streets. Still, I did no meth in jail. A lot of the whole withdrawal thing is psychological. People believe they'll get sick if they quit drugs and build it all up in their heads. Some get physically sick and throw up. Most get chills. I never had withdrawals. I quit heroin that way. In prison, I quit meth. I later did the same thing with cigarettes. I had smoked for 50 years. I bought two cartons of cigarettes a week before Thanksgiving, and I said, "I'm not buying anymore cigarettes. When these are gone, they are gone." I was smoking over two packs a day. I made those cartons last until New Year's. I had two cigarettes left New Year's Day. I said, "Well, I will smoke them right now and be done with it." I never had cravings.

People came to prison to score. The guards brought in heroin. They were getting paid off. I think the Aryan Brotherhood was taking care of it. One hit of heroin was $50. You got a hit from them, and they told you to call your guy on the outside. You called your guy on the outside and told him to deliver $50 cash to a certain address no later than three days from your phone call. If he didn't pay, you got beaten up in prison. You got hurt but usually got one more chance to have your people get the money to the right place. The ones who didn't either ended up in protective custody (PC) or got killed. Protective custody basically meant that guards put you into a super-maximum security, single-person cell. They brought you your meals there. You never got out. Snitches went into PC. If you were a troublemaker, you went into PC for a year or so; then you were sent to another prison. If you went to PC, everyone knew you were a rat or owed money, so you were not safe.

There were some nice guards. I always pretty much got along with all of them, except the ones who were really punks. A lot of them were corrupt because there were so many drugs coming into prison.

Like I said, prison is not what people always expect. People wonder about homosexuality in prison. I saw something happen one time. This

Apache kid came in and he was raped so badly he was put in the hospital. That night, a friend and I broke off the leg of a wooden table. We found the rapist and threw a blanket on him. Then we worked him over. They took him out in an ambulance the next morning.

The guys had girlfriends or wives or boyfriends, but it was very dangerous then to have an affair with a guy because of HIV. For a long time the homosexuals were segregated from other prisoners because of it. Well, they won a Supreme Court decision and were then allowed to mix with the general population. I remember going over to the medical clinic once. I spotted all the nurse's files, and I couldn't believe how many pink stickers were on the folders. I finally asked the guy, "What are the pink stickers for?"

He said, "Those are people who have AIDS and HIV. They're mostly gays, but if you get a prison tattoo from a dirty needle, you can get HIV."

I found out that about 50 percent of the population there had HIV because they'd used the same needles. Needles were hard to come by and were used to shoot heroin and make tattoos. I wasn't about to get a tattoo and walk out with AIDS. I did get prison ink, but it was with a brand new needle. I made sure I was the first person on it.

ORGANIZATION

MY TATTOO WAS THE SYMBOL OF AN ORGANIZATION I JOINED. It was an organization called The Silent Brotherhood, which was along the lines of the Aryan Brotherhood. They kept me alive the whole time I was at Douglas. We took care of business for the Aryan Brotherhood, like getting snitches and protecting our own. We did whatever it took. We were different from the Aryan Brotherhood, though. I didn't hate Jewish people. I've always respected Jewish people. As a matter of fact, I tried to volunteer during the Six Day War to go fight for them in Israel, but the war was over so quickly it never got off the ground. I didn't hate blacks. I didn't hate Hispanics. Close to half the prison population was black. There were many Hispanics. Our yard had about 600 people and only 140 were white. My organization ran the whites. The Black Muslims ran the blacks. The Mexican Mafia had two factions—the US Mexican Mafia and the *Mexican* Mexican Mafia. Now and then they went off against each other. Like I said, we didn't mix races. That was a great way to get killed. I saw it happen. You might get a beating, or you might get stabbed with a shiv.

Shivs could be made from anything, and everyone had a shiv. We made them out of wood by cutting a small piece and sharpening it with concrete. If you took concrete, you had to make sure you didn't get caught. We used the concrete to file down the wood. Then we wrapped a sock around the top to make a handle. I had one made of fiberglass and another made out of a can. My stash place was cool. There was a section of paneling on my wall and I was able to undo the screws. I managed to sneak a screwdriver from somewhere. I unscrewed the panel and put all my stuff in there. Then I put the panel back. The guards just searched the obvious places.

My cellmate was an enforcer with the Hell's Angels. Enforcers are the Angels' secret police. When there's a problem in the club and nobody can solve it, they send him in and he *carte blanche* does whatever it takes. If he has to kill a couple of people, he kills a couple of people. Pepe was his name. He was a white guy, but they called him

Pepe because he was five foot four, 90 pounds soaking wet, and like nitroglycerin. Mitchell Floyd Valentine was his real name. He'd fight anybody. Pepe was very well known by the FBI, and he was a Christian. Pepe and I ended up in protective custody for five months because we were under investigation by The United States Justice Department.

Pepe became a member of the Silent Brotherhood, too, and we rose in the ranks. When guards found out that Pepe and I were high-ranking members of the organization, they flipped out. The warden was convinced that we were sent there to kill him and his family. Pepe and I started out living at opposite corners of the prison, but we wound up being cellmates and the warden thought that was some kind of conspiracy. The warden did a walk-through at the prison once a month. One day he took one look at Pepe and then me and realized saw that we were in the first pod. The warden's face got red. He turned around and walked out and never did do his walkthrough in our pod. He was scared to death.

One day, I watched a guard walk down from the Wall. The Wall is where they did the death penalty. The guard was a lieutenant. He said, "So, you're the political prisoner?"

I said, "The warden doesn't know what he's talking about. If someone is supposed to kill him, it would be a lot easier to do on the streets than it would be in prison."

The guard said, "I know that, but the warden gets his head filled with stuff."

The Warden brought in the Justice Department. It was kind of like what the Gestapo was to Nazi Germany. They had never caught anybody as highly ranked as I was or as Pepe was. One Justice Department investigator was a lady. She came to interview me and brought a sergeant with her. The lady wouldn't talk to me. She whispered to the sergeant and the sergeant asked me questions. She was standing right there. I answered the sergeant as best I could, and then he turned around and whispered to her. I thought, *This is ludicrous. This is hilarious. She thinks that I am not allowed to talk to her or something.* It was funny. I started laughing. I couldn't help it. I realized that she thought I wouldn't talk to a woman. She had in her head that my organization saw women as breeders and nothing else.

The sergeant said, "You are in some serious trouble. She is the United States Justice Department, and she is doing a file on you."

I said, "Yes? Well, she can do all the files she wants on me. I've got nothing to hide."

He said, "It's not funny. You should stop laughing."

I said, "I'm laughing because this whole situation is ludicrous."

Even when I wasn't in PC, I was basically cut off from the outside world. I sent letters to family and brothers, and sometimes I called, maybe a couple of times a month. It was rough. They all lived so far away. My brothers were in the middle of the state, and I was in the opposite corner—about an eight-hour trip away. Plus, most of them were felons, so they couldn't come in to see me anyway. They weren't allowed. The whole time I was down there I had one visit. I think it was a Saturday before I was in maximum security. The prison had a little area with grills where people could barbecue. My friends brought in steaks, and we had a nice dinner.

I was all right, though, because I met plenty of interesting people at Douglas. One was a really level-headed guy, and I wondered, *What is he doing in prison*? He didn't belong in prison. He was a biker, too. I asked him his story.

He got invited up to Alaska by this club that runs Alaska. He was a cook and chemist and they wanted him to cook for them, BUT, part of the agreement was that he had to acknowledge the devil as his lord and savior. He wasn't a Christian, and he wasn't religious, but something about that rubbed him the wrong way. He told them, "I can't do that." They had him sitting on a chair surrounded by about 150 people, guys and girls. They all started chanting. Suddenly, he couldn't move. The crowd opened up and this black shadow started at one end of the building and came toward him. It got closer and closer and closer until it was just a few feet away. He freaked out. He told me that he knew then if the black thing touched him, he would be lost. He called out, "Jesus, please help me!"

The black thing receded right away and the girls screamed. Once he yelled for Jesus, he could move again. The people wanted to kill him, but the guy was under the club president's protection, since the president had invited him there. The president told the guy, "You leave here now. If I ever see you again, if any of us see you again, we will kill you on the spot. You need to go."

He told me, "I never believed in good and evil or God and the devil until I saw that shadow coming toward me. I knew inside of me that if that shadow touched any part of my body I would be lost. I don't know how or why I called out to Jesus."

He left Alaska and flew back down to California. I knew it wasn't baloney. That guy was telling me the truth. I never did ask him what he was in prison for, but I guessed probably drugs or maybe robbery. He was a hardcore biker, but he was clean cut. You never know who you will meet in prison.

SAVED

PRISON WAS THE BEST THING THAT EVER HAPPENED TO ME. It saved my life. I was doing so many drugs and bad dangerous things; I wouldn't have lasted. I figure I had a year left to live before I was sent to Douglas.

I'll never forget one day in prison. I was about to shave. I looked in the mirror. I stared into the mirror and came to the realization that when I was on that garbage, drugs, I was the kind of person I wanted nothing to do with. I was the kind of person my gang ran *out* of Flagstaff.

Three intense, important things happened to me in prison, and that moment started all of them. The first was I made a vow to never touch drugs again. The second was that I would get as much education there as possible. They had a college program. I signed up and studied electronic engineering and TV repair. The third thing was much bigger.

For two and a half years, Pepe kept trying to get me to go to the chapel. I laughed him off and used every excuse you could think up. I said stuff like, "I can't tonight because I'm taking my parakeet out for a walk," or, "I'm teaching my parakeet to swim." Then Pepe introduced me to Panama. Panama was a hitman for the Medellin Cartel. He was serving several life sentences. We became friends.

One day Pepe and Panama met me in the yard. Pepe said, "Big Bob, I love you like a brother, but you are going down. When I die I'm going to be in paradise."

Panama said, "Yeah Bob, the way you're going, you're going to the *caca* place." Those were his exact words. "You're going to the *caca* place." He meant hell.

Pepe said, "Bob, please come to the chapel with me tonight."

There was just so much sincerity in his words. It melted my heart, and I said, "All right, I'll come tonight, but don't expect a miracle."

Pepe and Panama immediately cracked up laughing.

"What? Did I say something funny?"

Pepe said, "You said 'don't expect a miracle.' This was the *last* time I was going to ask you to come to chapel. After two and a half years you finally said, 'yes.'"

I went to chapel. It wasn't what I expected it to be. There were 128 convicts in there from all different races. In prison you only hang out with your race, so I thought, *This is a good way to get killed.* Everybody in the chapel got along really well, even across racial lines, and I liked it, so I started going twice a week. We had this pastor named Tom Shields who drove down from Sierra Vista with his wife Dora. He was 95, and she was 90. They drove 60 miles one way to preach to us on Wednesday and Saturday nights.

I never wanted to do what I called the "Jesus thing," mostly because I smoked pot. I considered marijuana to be different from drugs, but I also thought that if I accepted Jesus as my savior and smoked pot, I would be a hypocrite. I knew when I got out of prison one of the first things I planned to do was put a big old stogie in my mouth. Well, Tom kept looking at me one night and finally came over. He said, "Excuse me, but I've got to tell you something."

"What's that?"

He said, "The Lord is telling me to tell you something."

I said, "Okay, let's hear it. What's He telling you to tell me?"

Tom said, "If you accept Jesus Christ as your Lord and Savior, and you smoke marijuana and cigarettes, God is not going to send you to hell."

I asked, "How do you know that's what I was thinking? I haven't told anyone." It was as stumbling block, a secret in my mind.

Tom said, "God knows every thought you have."

"Every thought I have? Man, I'm in big, big trouble."

Later, I told Pepe, "I can't do this Jesus thing."

Pepe asked, "Why not?"

I said, "Because, I've got something to do when I get out. I have to kill my ex-wife."

Pepe said, "That's okay. You can do that and then ask for forgiveness. You'll be forgiven."

I said, "Wait a minute Pepe. I don't know much of anything, but that doesn't sound right to me. That sounds like premeditated sin."

I took a walk on the track the next morning after breakfast. That was my time that I always prayed and talked to God. I said, "Jesus, I don't understand this forgiveness thing. All I have to do is repent of my sins and ask you for forgiveness and my whole past is wiped out? Everything is forgiven?"

His voice spoke. I remember looking around because it was a deep loud voice. It was coming from the speakers in the prison yard, coming up out of the ground, and out of the buildings! I wondered how nobody else there heard it.

I heard, "Child, how could you honestly expect to be forgiven of all your trespasses when you can't forgive the little trespasses that have been done against you?"

I sat down on a big block of concrete. I sat down there for about ten minutes trying to argue it out in my head, and I said, "You're right. How can I? How can I expect to be forgiven of so much when I can't forgive others? What do I do?" An invisible hand grabbed me and marched me down to my pod. I got a pen and paper, and I wrote, "Ronda, I forgive you." That would've been enough, but instead I wrote an eight-page letter. It was beautiful. It wasn't my writing.

I missed my children. The word I was getting from my brothers was that I'd probably never see them again. I just resigned myself to that. I prayed about it, and I just kind of blocked it out of my mind. Even now I don't think I will ever see them again.

I let Pepe read the letter and this Hell's Angel, this hardcore Hell's Angel, had tears coming down his eyes. He said, "This is the most beautiful letter I've ever read about asking someone to forgive you and you forgiving somebody. Man, the Holy Spirit has got his hand on you now." He could always tell. I mailed it off to Rhonda's last address. I knew then I couldn't kill her. I wished her a happy life.

At one point, I thought I was totally alone, and then I realized, *I'm not alone. Jesus loves me. He told me through that clerk in the Flagstaff store before I went down this road, and He* knew *the road I was going to go down. But there He was and here He is, telling me He loves me.*

One Saturday night Dora came alone to chapel and told us, "Tom is dying. His body is shutting down, and he was too uncomfortable to be here. Please pray for him."

The next day, for the first time in my life, I got down on my knees to pray. I said, "God, I got a deal for you. You spare that man, and I promise You if he comes back, when he does an altar call, I will go up. I will proclaim to the world that I belong to You. That's my promise. You have my word." Then I went about my business. That Wednesday night, who do you think was back at Douglas in the chapel? Tom Shields.

Right away I started squirming and thinking, *It might not be a good idea for me to go up there at the altar call. Tom might have a relapse from the shock.* It didn't matter what I thought. When Shields did the altar call, that invisible hand grabbed me by the ear and marched me to the altar. I told the world, "I belong to Jesus."

It felt good. *I* felt good. I knew I wasn't going to have to do bad stuff anymore. I accepted Jesus as my savior. I've never regretted it.

PAROLE

NOT LONG AFTER THAT, I WAS OFFERED PAROLE. I turned it down. I didn't even go to the board. They were trying to thin out the prison population because they were doing away with the parole system altogether. They had to get a lot of people out of there to make room because from then on whatever time you got, you were going to have to serve that.

When I was offered parole, I told the officers I had to go and pray about it. The counselor said, "You've got to what?"

I said, "I need to go pray about it."

He looked at me funny and said, "Okay."

I had only been saved for two weeks and worried that if I went out at that point I'd be back in a month in chains. I prayed, "Lord, I'm offered a parole. I don't know if I'm strong enough to resist the temptations that are going to be out there, or if I will just jump right back into the same guy I was before. I am asking for You to guide me and let me know what I should do." The thought I got was, *Don't go out now because you'll be back in 30 days in chains.* So, I turned down parole.

The counselor flipped out. He said, "Nobody turns down a parole."

I said, "There's a first time for everything."

He said, "Because you've been offered a parole and you've turned it down, you lose all your good time, and you have to serve every day of your sentence, which means you won't get out until 2006. Remember, the new rule is that there's no more parole."

I said, "This is God's will."

Three months later they called me over again. The counselor said, "You've been offered another parole. If you sign this paper you will go out day after tomorrow."

I said, "Wait a minute. You told me there were no more paroles."

He said, "There aren't, but the Governor and the head of Department of Corrections had a meeting about you and seven other guys. If you will sign the papers you all go home day after tomorrow."

I said, "Let me go pray about it."

He said, "Not again."

I said, "Yes, again." I prayed the same thing.

God said, "You are stronger now. You have grown in the Bible and you have grown in your faith. You are strong enough to resist the temptations now."

I signed the form, which put me on ten years of parole. I was to check in with my parole officer twice a month and get drug tested each time. I left prison on Easter Sunday of 1995.

OUT

THE FIRST DAY OUT OF PRISON IS STRANGE. You can't believe you're out. It's hard. It took me a couple months to get adjusted to being free again. I kept waiting for a cop to grab me and throw me back in again. I'd lost my right to vote, own property, have a passport, and possess a firearm.

I was sent to Tucson. I knew only one person there, a young lady. She let me stay at her place. I had to report to the parole officer on Monday. On Monday I told the parole officer, "I want to get paroled to Phoenix. I have people there I can stay with, and I know I can get work."

He said, "I want you to stay here. I like the guys who I think are going to make it." I explained over and over how I knew no one, and that I could better find work in Phoenix. I understood him, though. So many prisoners get paroled and end right back up in prison. He finally let me change locations. The brothers from Flagstaff came and got me and took me back home. I was there for a little while and working where I could in Phoenix.

On my birthday in '95, just three and a half months after being released, I walked into my Phoenix parole officer's office. He plopped a fat stack of papers down in front of me and said, "Happy birthday."

I thought, *Oh, no. I'm going to have to fill out all these papers.* I said, "What's this?"

He said, "You're all done, and I'm cutting you lose."

I was paranoid. I said, "What do you mean you're cutting me lose? You're putting me back in prison?"

He said, "No. You're done with parole."

I said, "I got ten years of parole."

He said, "No, I can cut you lose any time I want. I filed the paperwork. Stay clean for one year, and your rights will be restored, except your right to carry a firearm. You'd have to take that to Congress." I couldn't believe it, but he said, "You're going to make it. I can tell. I've been doing this long enough. I know if a person's going to make it or not. There's something different about you."

I served time from '90 to '95, plus the first 255 days. I was supposed to be out on parole until September of 2006. I think the difference was being a Christian. I believe my good outcome was from God because I was obedient. When He said to stay in jail, I did. God not only got me out when there was technically no getting out, but He also erased ten years of parole. I haven't been in trouble since.

COLORADO

I MOVED TO COLORADO. I had always wanted to go there. Crazy Brian hired me to guard his sister Kathy because there were some weird things going down with her. She and her husband had a million-dollar farming business, and they were getting a divorce. The husband hired private investigators to tail her. The couple got back together, but the husband never got rid of the private investigators. Kathy and I never knew anything about the investigators.

The couple decided to move all the way to Albuquerque, New Mexico. I stuck around there for a while to keep guarding Kathy for Brian. She and I pulled into a burger place one day. She said, "There they are. They are here now." She sounded afraid.

I said, "Who's here now?"

She said, "Nobody, nobody."

We drove around to a couple of other places. She said, "Oh, no. They are still following me."

I said, "Who is, Kathy?"

She said, "These people follow me all the time. Up in Colorado they followed me, but I didn't think they would come to New Mexico." We drove back to Colorado, and we went into a Radio Shack. I hadn't even planned on going there. Kathy and I weren't in that store two minutes before the store's phone rang, and it was her husband calling her at Radio Shack.

It freaked her out because she never knew the husband had hired people to follow her in the first place. I said, "All right, here's what we're going to do. I want you to drive down that narrow street over there. I'm going to jump out of the car. You lock the door immediately. I'm going to run these people down. I'll find out who they are and what they want." I said, "They'll find out what big Bob is all about." I said it all really loudly so the men could hear. Well, as soon as I did, they turned around and left. I got their license number and had it run. It turned out it belonged to a 90-year-old squaw on a reservation. Those investigators were bad. They had her car bugged. I knew it. I know evil when I see it.

We found out who they were, but they never bothered Kathy again after that. Kathy and her husband divorced, and she moved back to Colorado.

Kathy had three sons. I stayed with her and her sons in a house in Colorado. We found pentagrams drawn on the floors and walls and found tiny bones of animals. We learned that kids used to break into the house and do animal sacrifices. It was a weird house, and at night we heard strange noises and people talking.

I talked to the pastor of the church I went to there, and he said, "Get the whole family together and walk through the house to every window and every doorway. Anoint the windows and doors in oil. Rebuke Satan out and ask God to guard the family with angels so the demons can't come in again. I was always the last one to bed, so that night I checked all the doors. Everything was locked up. In my bed, as soon as I lay down, I heard voices talking. I got up and went out in the living room, and the rocking chair was rocking, but there was nobody there. I got back in bed. I was lying facing the window and all of a sudden I heard another voice. I looked at the window, and there were two red glowing globes about a foot apart and a black shadow at the window.

It was a demon saying, "You will never belong to Jesus. You belong to me; I have my mark on you." I could see it and feel its three claws touching my arm and burning right to the bone. I was so scared, and I am not a person who gets scared. I was petrified. I usually kept a gun under my pillow, but after prison I didn't have one anymore. Normally, I would have grabbed that gun and blown a hole through the window. Finally, I just called on Jesus like the guy in prison had up in Alaska. I yelled, "Jesus, please help me!"

I heard Jesus laughing. He said, "Child, what are you afraid of? He has no power. He can't even come in here unless you invite him in. Why are you afraid?"

I realized that and said, "Get thee gone Satan! Get thee gone!" It went away.

I used to get up around five o'clock in the morning there in Colorado. I would make myself a cup of coffee and sit in the front room. That room was all glass. I could look down across the canyon and watch bears, deer, elk, and an eagle. There was a lake, too. The eagle would fly down and catch fish. On Saturday, three days after I'd seen Satan at my window, I was sitting there watching for the eagle when I remembered something my grandmother said to me way back in 1954.

I was seven years old and had a new truck. I wanted to go out and play with it, but the weather was bad. It was raining hard and had been for a long time. I asked my grandmother, "Grandma, how come it's raining so much?"

She thought about it and said, "Okay, you really want to know?"

I said, "Yes."

She said, "Each raindrop is a tear from Jesus because somebody sinned."

I don't know why I had that particular memory right there in that front room in Colorado, but I suddenly realized my sin had caused a great flood. I broke down, and I cried like I have never cried before or since. For the next almost 36 hours it was uncontrollable. I couldn't stop. Kathy said to me, "Bob, stop. It's okay."

I said, "It needs to happen." She kept the children away. I cried all day Saturday, Saturday night, and I missed church on Sunday morning. Around four o'clock Sunday afternoon I stopped.

Kathy said, "Do you want to go to church tonight?"

I said, "Yes, as long as my face isn't too puffy from all the crying."

She said, "No, you're fine."

I told Kathy not to tell anybody what happened, and she didn't.

I went to church. Our pastor was in San Diego at a Promise Keepers convention, so his wife led our service. Right in the middle of her praise and worship, she stopped singing and called me up front. She put her hand on my beard and said, "Your face is beautiful."

I said, "Sister, you're as blind as a bat because there isn't anything beautiful about this face."

She said, "That not what I said, and besides, there are people here who would argue with you. No, I said your *faith* is beautiful. Your sins are washed away by your tears of repentance and by the blood of Jesus Christ. Your sins no longer exist." How she knew I was going through that, I don't know. Up to that point I had never felt clean, but after crying those many hours and hearing her words, I felt like a new person. I felt clean *inside.*

She said, "The Holy Spirit told me to tell you to read the book of Job."

I said, "Okay." Job lost everything on a bet God made with the devil. I started reading about how God knew Job was righteous, and Job suffered at the hands of the devil anyway. God was proving that we should love Him and trust Him no matter what. Job lost everything, but he still refused to do evil. By the time I read the second chapter I was dancing. I thought, *I don't have problems. This man Job had problems.*

I grew up Catholic, with Mom hoping I'd be good, but I stayed out of church. I could have been so much better, but I stayed away from God and wasted most of my life. Since I accepted Jesus Christ as my Lord and Savior, I've never regretted it, and I have never walked away. I never will.

Now I'm getting to the age and situation when He's going to take me home. I just pray every day that I'm right with Him, and if I've done anything wrong and don't know what it is, He will show me what I've done wrong so I can pray about it, end it, and ask forgiveness.

Colorado was good for me. The little town where I lived is called Dolores. It's about 60 miles from Four Corners, down on the southwest corner of the state. The population was about 800. I was still helping Kathy, but I also set up a TV repair shop. I learned the skills in prison.

In prison school I got paid ten cents an hour for just going to school. Eventually, I had completed three semesters when the jail officials realized I didn't have a high school diploma. A deputy warden said, "You can't have all these credits." Well, I'd gone to school on the streets, too, so I had over a hundred credits total. I think when I finally finished, I had 131 credits, which back then was enough for an associate's degree. Anyway, the deputy warden said, "You can't have these credits. Did you lie about going to high school?"

I said, "No. The instructors all asked me the year of my graduation, and my graduation year was the class of 1966."

He said, "Did you actually graduate?"

I said, "No. I had to quit just shy of graduation to take care of my sister and brother."

He kept on, "You can't have these credits."

I said, "Fine. Give me back all my time, and we'll call it square."

He said, "We can't do that."

I said, "Right. Then you can't take my credits away."

He said, "You have to at least go take the GED."

I said, "Okay. I will." They sent me over the next day to take the pre-test, which should last one full day and part of the next morning. Well, I had it done before lunch. I started at eight in the morning and had the whole test done by eleven o'clock.

The deputy looked at it and said, "You didn't have to study anything?"

I said, "Well, no, it's just a high school test." Two weeks later, I took the real GED. Again, I had it done by the end of the morning. I had to write a fiction story, and they really liked the story. The test administrators told me, "You should be an author." I laughed. Man, I hate writing. I hate writing, but I got my GED. Then I had all my credits, and I finished my classes in prison.

I wanted to get into business machine repair because my instructor told me, "Those are the guys who make the money—the guys who work on the cash registers. They get $2,500 for a service call, just for showing up. And, they schedule four or five of them on the same day. Then on top of that they get whatever it costs to fix the machines."

I asked, "That's legal?"

He said, "Yes, that's legal."

I said, "Man, I'm going to get into that."

He said, "You have to do the TV repair first, and then you can go into the business machine repair."

Unfortunately, due to budget cuts, as soon as I graduated from TV repair they cut the business machine education program. I took courses that went toward electronic engineering. Plus, before, when I worked for the state, they gave me 200 hours of college level stuff for preventative maintenance, engineering, building roads, and things like that. I had a lot of credits.

When I started my little TV repair business, I was really busy for about three months. I fixed every TV in town, even some big screen TVs in bars, as well as audio systems. Then I starved for the next three months. I wound up sitting there feeling sorry for myself and Christine, my sister Joni's oldest daughter, called me out of the blue. We'd been writing for years. She wrote to me when I was in prison, but we never actually spoke on the phone. Of all the states, Colorado was my favorite. I liked the wide open spaces and the way people were. It was a friendly state to live in and people were really nice to me, but Christine's phone call made me miss home.

NEW HAMPSHIRE

MY EYESIGHT GOT SO BAD I COULDN'T WORK ON SMALL ELECTRONIC PANELS ANYMORE. I was frustrated and homesick, so in 1996 I went back east to see Mom and visit Joni and her husband Paul. They were living in New Hampshire. It's a miracle I could even get there because I had no money to buy a plane ticket. My sister Joni had raised five kids and didn't really have any money either, but she pulled off a miracle. She had a credit card for a department store called Filene's Basement. She remembered seeing a sign in the store that said you could book travel arrangements there through an agent of some kind. She called the customer service number and told the clerk that she had a brother who wanted to fly home from Colorado. The clerk let her use her department store credit card to buy me a plane ticket. Normally, they didn't do that, and the clerk actually said she'd never done it before. To Joni and me, that meant that God wanted me to fly east. It was a round-trip ticket. I did plan to go back to Colorado.

I visited Mom and stayed with Joni and Paul. Joni asked, "Why don't you stay for David's high school graduation?" He was the youngest of the five kids. I did. Then she said, "You might as well stay for your birthday." I stayed for my birthday, then something else, then something else. By the time I was ready to go back west, the ticket had expired, and we couldn't get a refund.

My niece Sara got into a wreck and brought her car to me. I've been an auto mechanic all my life. She'd taken her little car to a guy in town, and he was going to sock it to her with the insurance deductible and all the extra stuff, so she asked me if I could fix her car. I said, "Yes. I can fix it. I'll straighten out what I can, replace what I can't straighten out, and paint it." I used Paul's tools. When I finished, the car looked good. Sara paid me the money her insurance company gave her, but I said, "Too much. Too much."

She said, "No. You take it and buy yourself some tools." I did. I bought a bunch of tools and set up shop.

I was still living with Paul and Joni, but needed my space, so after working hard and saving a little, I bought a small camper, then a bigger camper, and then the motor home I have now.

I worked on cars and made a decent living. One day, I was under a car and a big, big snake crawled right over my belly. He was six feet long. I felt him because my shirt was up. I yelled and sat up and smacked my head on the frame of the car, almost knocking myself out. I reached out and grabbed that snake and threw him as hard as I could. He hit the wall and disappeared after that. By that time, I'd had my fair share of snake encounters.

My first spring in Arizona I killed all those rattlesnakes right around the house. Then when I was working the roads, a rattlesnake bit me right through the tongue of my boot. We were working on old Highway 66. It was in the middle of the summer, and the truck I was driving had a blown head gasket. Every few hours I had to stop and put water in it. We broke for lunch. Afterward, I put water in the gasket, got in the truck, and went back to hauling stuff. Later that night my coworker called me and said, "After you pulled out there was a rattlesnake right where you were standing when you put water in the gasket."

I said, "I think he might have bitten me because my leg feels really funny and tired." I took my boot off, and I could see two strip marks on the top of my foot. The fangs penetrated just enough to get a little poison into my foot. I threw the boots away. Another time, Lil and I were down at Lake Havasu, sitting across the lake from my favorite camp spot. I was hanging out and smoking a joint in the middle of the night. All of a sudden I felt something slide over the top of both my feet at the same time. I thought, *That's a snake. That's a BIG snake.* Then it dawned on me, *That's probably a rattlesnake!* I let out a yell.

Lil said, "What's the matter?"

I yelled, "Snake!" I jumped up on the picnic table. I never saw it, but I know it was there. I've seen rattlesnakes, copperheads, water moccasins, and one Arizona coral snake. The coral snake was about as big around as a pinky finger and only twelve to fourteen inches long. The difference with those snakes is they have molars, not fangs, kind of like a Gila monster. He has to chew the poison in. There's no anti-toxin for the venom. Back on the road crew, we had a pet Gila monster up in the rocks. We worked that area for about a month. We fed him pieces of sandwiches every day. Gila monsters aren't aggressive unless you corner them. Every day we'd sit on the same rocks, and he'd come down low to get his snack.

I had some real fun and some real trouble out west. Those years turned into strong memories. I never returned to live out there again.

BAPTIZED

I NEEDED TO GET WATER BAPTIZED. After a year or more in New Hampshire, around October of 1997, I decided to get baptized by immersion. I was attending a Calvinist church, a congregational church, in Grafton, New Hampshire. The pastor Tom and I got along really well.

Family and some friends all met up at Canaan Street Lake. It was in the evening when we went. Pastor Tom was only about five-foot-four. He waded into the water, and because he was so short compared to me, he had to get almost up to his chest in the water. He kept asking, "Big Bob, will you just kneel down in the water?"

I did the best I could. He said, "I baptize you in the name of the Father, the Son, and the Holy Spirit." It was cold outside, maybe 30 or 40 degrees, and after the pastor dipped me under that water, we were both freezing. We almost turned blue it was so cold. The people had brought extra towels and blankets. They wrapped us up right away. Then we all went to the pastor's house and just sat by the fire the rest of the evening. It was a good experience. I think the lake froze up the next month.

FIRE

I THINK I ATTRACT FIRE AS MUCH AS I ATTRACT SNAKES. Even though I am saved and different in so many ways, I guess I'm still me, no matter what. My great niece was up from Oregon. She smoked, and she thought she put her cigarette out, but she didn't. She just knocked the ash off it. That coal went off in the dry fall leaves, but she had no idea because she'd gone off on a hike. Paul was in the front of the house, so I yelled, "Paul, call 911! There's a small fire in the backyard!"

He thought I was joking. He said, "Yeah, right. Well, let it burn. Maybe get some hamburgers and hot dogs out there."

I said, "No, Paul. I am serious. There's a fire going on in the backyard. I'm going to go up and try to put it out, but you need to call the fire department. Come on and have a look out the back window."

He said, "I'll look, but I know you are pulling my leg." We looked out the back window and the whole backyard was on fire. He panicked, "What do I do?"

I said, "Call 911 like I told you." I grabbed the shovel and ran a hose up and turned the water on. I started cutting a fire line and kept cutting all the way around the brush. Then I shoveled dirt and hit the brush with the hose. I'd about had it when the fire department showed up. I was standing in a lot of smoke, so they put me in the ambulance.

A fireman said, "You know, it's a good thing you were on this fire. How many people did you have helping you?"

I said, "Just me."

He said, "You did really good." They kept me in that ambulance and on oxygen for 30 minutes because I'd swallowed a lot of smoke.

My great niece came back down the hill and asked, "What happened down here?"

I said, "There was a fire here." Then she figured it out right away. I said, "The cigarette wasn't out, but the fire is." I didn't tell the fire department anything.

LICENSE

I SEEM TO ALSO ATTRACT MIRACLES. When I got out of jail, I had so many speeding tickets from the past that I worried I'd never get my driver's license again. I almost always outran the police on my bike. When I was released, I had $14,000 in tickets and fines against my driver's license. After I moved to New Hampshire, I really needed to be able to drive, but Arizona wouldn't help me. I even got a state senator, through a friend of mine, to work on it. No one made any progress. I even talked to the lady who was the head of the Arizona Department of Motor Vehicles. I said, "Look, some of those fines were dismissed. I know it. I need you to just look up my records and see."

She said, "No you've got to pay the $14,000."

I called her every week and after a while, she wouldn't talk to me. One day, I was working on a car and thinking about the problem. I was underneath the car and God spoke to me. He said, "Are you ready to get out of My way and give Me the time to deal with your driving?"

I said, "Yes, Lord. What do You want me to do?"

He said, "Just make your call every Friday and that's it. Don't do anything else."

I said, "Okay."

My down-the-road neighbor was a disabled Massachusetts state trooper, and he was a Mennonite. He asked me about my license. I told him, "God spoke to me today." This was on a Tuesday.

"What did He say?" he asked. I told him what God said to me.

The trooper looked surprised and asked, "He said that to you?"

I said, "Yes."

He said, "Okay, I want to see what God's going to do."

Thursday came. Around noon I was underneath another car and God said, "You need to go and call Arizona."

I said, "Lord, it's Thursday. It's not Friday. I call on Fridays."

"You need to go and call right now," He commanded me.

I said, "All right." I got up and called the Arizona DMV. I got that lady who didn't want to talk to me on the phone.

She said, "You. What do you want?"

I said, "You know what I want. I want you to check my status and see what I've got to do."

She said, "You know what it's going to say."

I heard her punch up the computer and all of a sudden she gasped, "Oh, my God. Oh, my God."

I said, "What? What's the matter?"

She said, "The $14,000—it's not on your license anymore."

I said, "What are we going to do?"

She said, "You have one $500 ticket you need to pay. Pay that, send a $25 reinstatement fee, and we'll mail you your driver's license."

I paid the ticket and the fee. They sent me my Arizona license. For some reason when I was going to go take the New Hampshire test I thought, *I'd better call New Hampshire, too, just to make sure everything is square.*

I called them up, and I gave them my name. The guy said, "Wait a minute, you have a fine here under a different name in Arizona." It was an alias that I had used. How anyone knew about that alias was a mystery. Arizona didn't even know it was me. The guy said, "It's you. We know it's you. You've got to pay the ticket."

I asked for the docket number, and I called Arizona up again. The lady said, "No. You're record is clean."

I said, "Look under this docket number under this name."

She did and said, "Is that you?"

I said, "Yes, that was an alias I used. How much is the fine?"

I didn't have the money to pay it at that time. What's weird is that I got a bus repair job that same afternoon that paid me *exactly* what I needed. I sent in the money. Then I got my New Hampshire license.

I liked being back to normal and with family. By that time, my sister had left Paul, so it was just Paul and me living there on the property unless one of the kids was visiting. I won't go into all that because it's my sister's business, but I will say that our childhood was part of the problem. I love my sister, and I loved Paul just like a brother. I called him my brother. He was good to me.

I did the cooking for Paul, and I used to make my mom's potato pancakes. I was cooking up a whole mess of them for dinner one night. My niece was staying at the house with Paul and Joni. Her husband had just left her for a younger girl. The ex-husband came up to get their son and brought the girlfriend with him. That was just wrong. You don't bring your girlfriend around your ex-wife, especially to get your kid. No class. No class at all. Anyway, I was making potato pancakes. The ex-husband said, "What are you cooking?"

I said, "Potato pancakes."

He said, "What? What kind of pancakes?"

"Potato pancakes. You want to try one?" I was trying to be polite.

He said, "Yes, I'll try one."

I set them out. The ex-husband and his girlfriend wound up sitting there, and they ate about a half a dozen each. I thought it was weird, but I was nice for my niece's son's sake.

RIPPED

PEOPLE ARE FUNNY. At the Grafton church I was going to (not the one I go to now) the treasurer asked me to do some work on a truck for him. It was stranded in the middle of a field in the summertime. He had a shop out there on that field. I said, "Leave the shop unlocked so I can get a drink of water and use the facilities." He didn't. I worked out there on his truck for almost two weeks. I explained to him everything that was wrong with the vehicle. I had to rebuild the air brake system, intake manifold, and gaskets. It was a whole bunch of work, so I ran up $700 in parts alone. When it was all done, I called him on the phone and gave him the total bill amount. Then I said, "Once you put 500 miles on it, bring it back because I have to re-torque everything."

Well, he came back one day, and I said, "You come down to pay me my money?"

He said, "I'm not paying you nothing."

I asked, "What do you mean you're not paying me?"

He said, "I had to take it somewhere to get everything re-torqued."

I said, "I told you that to begin with. After 500 miles you were supposed to bring it to me so I could re-torque it."

He said, "Well, you didn't finish the work."

I just shook my head.

I had a witness. I was using this lady's phone, and her husband was on the board of directors at the church. She was right there when I called him with the invoice amount and told him to bring the truck back after 500 miles. Still, he never paid me. He burned me. I didn't care that much for my labor, but $700 in parts? I had to go in and talk to my supplier, Parts House, and explain the situation. I said, "It's going to take me a little while to pay it off, but I will pay it off." And I did.

That church treasurer guy went into Parts House right after that. The owner was there. He looked him up one side and down the other. You see, the owner knew me. He refused to sell the treasurer the parts. He said, "What? You're going to rip somebody else off now? Just can't stop?"

The treasurer got real mad. He complained to the church leadership. They came over and talked to me, and I said, "I did this work because you guys vouched for him. I heard rumors he didn't like to pay his bills, so I asked you, Tom. You're the pastor of the church. You said, 'No. He may take a while, but he will pay his bill.' I did the work, and he burned me. I'm coming to you as the Bible says to do and to see what you're going to do about it."

He said, "We'll have a meeting." So they had a meeting, and Tom wouldn't even come back to talk to me. He sent a deacon back to talk to me.

The deacon said, "This is what we decided you have to do. You have to forget about the whole thing and not mention it to anybody."

I said, "So, in other words, what you're saying is you're going to cover it up for him, and you don't want me telling anybody that he ripped me off, and I just have to pay his car's bill and everything else. That's what you're telling me, right?" He didn't say anything. Churches need to be careful how they treat members because I lost a lot of respect for those men for not making the car guy do what was honest and right. I left that church.

TATTOOS

I KNOW WHAT KIND OF PERSON I WAS AND WHAT KIND OF PERSON I AM NOW. My tattoos remind me. I got my first one when my gang was on a run. I was drunk and don't remember it. My wife at the time, Rhonda, bought it for me. I woke up in the middle of the night because my arm felt tight and it hurt. I touched my arm, and it was wet. When I turned on the light, I saw blood on my hand. Immediately, I jumped up and got my pants on and grabbed my pistol. Rhonda woke up and said, "What are you doing?"

I said, "Somebody stabbed me in my arm."

She asked, "Where'd they stab you?"

I said, "They stabbed me in my arm. It's all bloody."

Rhonda said, "Oh, no. I bought you a tattoo."

I said, "What?" Immediately, I ripped the bandage off, and the first thing I saw was her name on there. You don't put somebody's name on you unless it's your mom's or your kid's. I said, "Who did this?"

She said, "Inks and Art in Tucson."

I said, "What were we doing in Tucson? We were supposed to be up in Colorado."

She said, "You were high. We ended up in Tucson, and I bought you that."

I said, "YOU put your name on me?"

She said, "Yeah, I wanted that."

Man, I must have blacked out. I later got a cover-up tattoo. It is a game board. It represents the games that people play. A biker brother of mine had opened up a tattoo parlor in Flagstaff. I was staying at the clubhouse. The brother came in one day at about three in the morning. I'd had about all I could handle with that name on my arm, and I had a poker in the wood stove. I pulled it out white hot, and I was *just* getting ready to put it on my arm to burn that tattoo off. He yelled, "What are you doing?!"

I said, "I'm getting rid of this cancer on my arm. I can't handle it on there anymore.

He said, "Oh, no, don't do that. I'll cover it up." He set up right there and started the first part of work on it that night. He planned to finish in a few days, but he violated his parole and police took him back to San Quentin. So, the tattoo is part gameboard and the rest is black. He was going to put flags on the black part.

I've got a big IMO (In Memory Of) tattoo on my left forearm with the names of the four brothers I've now lost—my two physical brothers Donnie and Paul and two who were like brothers, Joni's husband Paul and Rhonda's father Papa Mike. Above that I've got a self-portrait of me on a chopper going full-speed down the road. I've got another tattoo that's also covered up because it came from my prison gang. It was that group's symbol. That really wasn't me. A friend of mine who runs a tattoo parlor down in Massachusetts covered it up for me. She didn't charge me anything for it. The old tattoo was a hate symbol, but the new tattoo is a cross because that's who I am now.

My current pastor Bruce had some friends up recently, and I got to sit with them. Bruce told them a little about me, and they said, "This guy would never hurt anybody."

Bruce said, "You should have met him twenty years ago."

JESUS

SPEAKING OF MEETING STRANGE PEOPLE, I MET JESUS A FEW YEARS BACK. It was a weird situation. It started off in a dream. In the dream, it just so happened I was painting the old bar I had with Lil in Kingman. I was up on a ladder. All of a sudden I collapsed up on the ladder. My legs were draped over a rung and I was hanging upside down. The next thing I knew I was in a totally gray world. The sky was gray. The ground was gray. Everything was perfectly flat. In the very center of it was an upside-down tornado, a giant vortex. Where it went into the clouds there were lightning bolts. I was slowly being drawn to it. All the way around me people were being drawn to it. Some people were laughing and happy and having a ball, and other people were petrified. The children were pulling their parents by their hands. The children were happy and saying, "Come on, Mommy. Come on, Daddy."

A few days after the experience, I went to a lady who interprets dreams. She said that the happy people were the ones who knew Jesus and understood that they were going up to be judged. They weren't afraid at all to go up. The people who knew the truth and had been witnessed to and rejected Jesus are the ones who were afraid. She said, "Those people said no to Jesus, so they are going to get express tickets going the wrong way." The children were all happy because they were the age of innocence. The Bible states that any child the age of innocence is admitted into heaven.

So, back to the dream, the next thing I knew I looked down, and I was no longer on the gray road. I was on a path of pure red soil. It was green on both sides of the trail I was walking. On the left side was a little gully that went up into beautiful, beautiful trees, all green and brown. On the right, flowing along, was the purest water you've ever seen. I looked up ahead of the trees, and there was a man sitting up there wearing a brown leisure suit with a sweater. He was staring at me. He said, "Hello. It's about time you got here." He said, "I've been waiting and waiting for you to come by here." I looked at him closely and noticed that he had holes in his hands, and he wasn't wearing shoes. There were holes in his feet. The whole side of his sweater was wet. It was darker in color than the rest of his clothes. Then I realized, *I'm talking to Jesus.*

I said, "It's You, Lord! It's You! I'm finally with You!"

He said, "Yes, it's Me, but I have to send you back. It's not your time yet."

I said, "What do You mean You have to send me back? I want to be with You!"

He said, "You will be. I promise. Wait until you see the place I've prepared for you. You're going to love it, but for now I need you to go back because there are things I need you to do. Others could do them, but not in the way you're going to do them, and that is how I want them done."

I remember begging, "Please don't send me back, Lord. I want to be with You."

He said, "I promise you will be, but I need you to go back and do something for Me."

He gave me three messages to give to three different people. With two of the people, he put their names right on me.

Then he said, "For the third one, it's going to be a while. You're not going to remember the message or who it is for until you meet this person, but it will all be made clear in your mind. The other two, you will know right away and deliver the messages to them. Remember, you are just a messenger boy. You are delivering *My* messages to them. You had better go back now."

I said, "Okay, Lord."

I woke up sitting in my bed and bawling like a baby. I was back at my house. The next night, I had the same dream. The night after that, I had the same dream. All three were identical. Word for word. On the fourth day, I was outside sitting on my front deck. All of a sudden, I was in a vision.

Shortly after that time, I was getting counseling up in Lebanon, New Hampshire. The doctors had put me on Prozac, and I turned out to be highly allergic to it. I called Joni at three in the morning. She and Paul came and somehow got me out into her van and took me to the emergency room. I remember the room vividly. I had seen it in my vision. Plus, the same people I had seen in the vision were in that emergency room. It blew me away! I knew I would be okay. I knew the Lord would send me back. I recognized everything in the room. I could tell you who was coming in next and who was leaving, the whole nine yards. I had never been to Dartmouth-Hitchcock Medical Center before that night Joni and Paul took me, but when I got there I said, "Oh, I've been in this room. A police officer is going to come walking in here and then be standing by that table there."

Joni said, "How do you know?"

I said, "Because I've already seen all this."

She freaked out when a policeman walked in and stood by the table.

The doctors said my reaction to Prozac was life-threatening. They gave me shots of antihistamine and cut me loose in the morning. I was fine after that. I just didn't take Prozac anymore.

Then I followed the orders Jesus had given me in the dream. The first person to get a message was my old pastor, Tom. I said "Tom, I need to talk with you. There's something I have to tell you, but I want you to realize it's not from me. This is from the Lord." I told him about the dreams and vision. Then I told him what the Lord had said. I delivered the Lord's message.

That same afternoon, I met with the second gentlemen who I was supposed to talk to. I told him the message, and he looked at me like I was having a '60s drug moment, a flashback or something. He was having a hard time finding work. I was told to tell him, "Hang in there a little longer. Don't have faith in man. Have faith in the Lord. He is going to bless you with a job that's going to take you overseas. In my vision I heard that you're going to catch something and bring it back with you. Be careful over there. If you put your faith and trust in the Lord, you'll be okay." He looked at me like I was crazy.

Neither one of those men really believed me. I could tell. When I talked to each one of those guys, all the things I was supposed to tell them were fresh. The sentences popped into my mind like I'd just heard them. It took no effort. I told both of them, "Remember, the message is not from me. It is from God. It is from our Lord. I am just transferring a message that He put in my mind to give to you. Don't think I'm anything special because I'm not. I'm just the messenger boy."

About a month later, Tom came to me and said, "Everything you told me to expect happened exactly the way you said it was going to." Then Tom turned away from God, and he ripped the church off financially.

The other man got hired by the Federal Emergency Management System (FEMA) as a district head. He was sent to the Philippines and Thailand. He stayed over that way quite a while and caught some rare, exotic disease. There was no cure for it. It took over a year for doctors to figure out what it was. He wound up having to go on oxygen. Now they've got a treatment for him.

Many months later, at that church, all the elders and deacons and trustees were in the pastor's office. They called me in there. The second guy I had talked to led the questioning. He looked at me and asked, "Who *are* you?"

I said, "Me?"

He said, "Yeah, who are you?"

I said, "First off, you're giving me credit for something I don't deserve credit for. All I did was relay a message to you from the Lord. I had nothing to do with it. He told me to tell you this."

He said, "But who *are* you?"

I said, "I'm the same Big Bob I was yesterday. I'm me. The same guy you've known for a few years."

He said, "But how did you know? How did you know the stuff you told me? EVERYTHING happened just the way you said it would. How did you know that?"

I said, "I was sharing a message that the Lord put on my heart to tell you. Jesus doesn't lie. When Jesus tells you something, that is what it's going to be."

That was a bizarre meeting, but the situation was basic. The Lord gave me messages. I delivered them. Nothing more than that. Nothing less than that. A path was designed, and I followed it.

FORGIVING

I'M BEING THE BEST CHRISTIAN I CAN BE. That means forgiving others as I have been forgiven. After Rhonda, I started with my mom. She was a good mom. She had problems, but she did the best she could. I wasn't mad at her growing up, but I got very upset with her at one time because she said something to me that really hurt deep. One reason I returned east and stayed was because I knew I had to come back and make it right and forgive her. I wasn't able to do it, though, until the night she died. Doctors discovered she had cancer, and they put her in the hospital, and two weeks later she was dead. It was very, very fast. The cancer was all through her insides.

I was standing outside her hospital, and I was praying hard. Finally, I let it go. I forgave her. I told Jesus, "Lord, I feel like the weight of the world has been lifted off of me." I started dancing. People were driving by, probably asking, "Who's that crazy guy?"

She died that night.

What she said really hurt, and I don't talk about it. I kept it bottled up. I knew I had to let it go. A parent can hurt you more than anybody. She said the thing to me in 1983. I forgave her in 2004.

At her funeral, I stood up and sang "Amazing Grace" for her, and I broke down in the middle of it. My nieces Sara and Laura came up on either side of me and gave me support. It was six verses, but it was for Mom. She was worth it.

When her obituary was published, my friend Saul, who I loved like a brother, realized that I was still alive. We had lost contact since 1970. For decades, I thought he was dead. He thought I was dead. He drove up and found me.

CHURCH

I WENT TO A STRANGE LITTLE CHURCH FOR A WHILE. It was before I met Bruce. In that strange little church, there were discrepancies between what the pastors and I believe. They believed that once you receive salvation you can never lose it, and only 144,000 people are going to be saved in the whole world, and that doesn't match up with scripture at all. I asked them, "What you're saying is that if I'm going to hell then I had never had salvation to begin with, but the Bible says you can have salvation and lose it."

The pastor said, "Well, I've never seen that in the Bible."

I said, "I'll show you." I found three passages—one in Isaiah, one in Matthew, and one in Revelation. They said the same thing; you can be saved and then backslide and lose your salvation.

He said, "We'll have to have a study about that," but he never talked about it again. He wanted to hush me up.

I said, "I can't go to this church. You're teaching against scripture."

I tried an Assembly of God, and they hired a new pastor. He was bizarre. I'll never forget the day that he had the whole body in there, and he said, "I need anybody who is standing behind me to cross this line and stand up here."

There were three of us (Dale, Eric, and me) behind him. We were loading up equipment, not talking about God or anything else, really, but that pastor wanted us to stand beside him like we worshipped him or something. We walked out of the church. Then he got really squirrelly. Elders of the church had meetings, and everybody in the congregation got an opportunity to talk to them. It turned out the guy was embezzling from their church fund. He was a pathological liar. The elders didn't give up on him, though. They told him to go to this counseling thing in Ohio. He said, "What if I don't?"

They said, "Then we're going to strip you of your pastoral credentials. You will no longer be a pastor."

He went twice. After the second time he came back and said, "They can't teach me anything," and refused to go again.

My church now is doing well. Pastor Bruce Jerome took over many years ago and did a great job. Paul attended there with me. Bruce is retiring, and I will miss him. Bruce has helped me so much in my faith. He and his wife Gracie have mentored me and taught me how to behave as a Christian. Bruce worked as a policeman his whole life while he was also serving as a pastor. I really will miss him. He wrote a book of devotionals, and the March 16 one discusses Christian friendship. He writes about how close our friendship is even though he was a policeman for decades while I was a criminal. Pastor Bruce has been good.

I had another miracle not long ago. We had a prophetic evangelist up from Virginia. John Chacha was his name. He immigrated into the United States. He is a very high up prophetic evangelist in the church. My eyesight was really bad from the diabetes. I could barely see. John Chacha came up to me and said, "God is going to heal your eyes, Bob. You have to have faith."

I said, "John, I have the biggest mustard seed you've ever seen." I have faith a lot bigger than a mustard seed. I know that God can do whatever God is going to do.

John and other church brothers anointed my eyes in oil, had me close them, count to three, and open them. Three days later I was lying in bed and I woke up, opened my eyes, and saw clearly. It blew me away. My vision was crystal clear. I just sat there and said over and over, "Wow. Wow. Wow." That was on a Wednesday. Friday I went to see the eye doctor. She did the examination and then stared at me for several minutes.

Finally, she said, "Bob, if I hadn't treated you before, and if I didn't know you, I would say you were trying to pull a fast one on me."

I said, "Why, what's going on?"

She was, "Not only has your vision improved, but also there is not even evidence in your eyes that you have diabetes."

I said, "I had someone anoint my eyes."

She said, "Well, I have heard of miraculous healings, but this is the first time I've ever actually seen one. Your vision is back to normal, and your eyes are one of the first organs diabetes attacks."

I had 20/13 vision up until I got diabetes. I used to be driving down the road with somebody, and a mile away I could read the street signs because when I was looking at something that was twenty feet away, it appeared like it was only thirteen feet away. I could look at the ground, and it was like I was looking at it through a magnifying glass. When friends lost stuff they'd always get me to walk around the area and find it. Earrings, little tiny things, I could see them as plain as day. The doctor was totally blown away by my healing and wrote it down in my charts. She said there was no logical explanation. She said it had to be a miraculous healing.

When I feel good, I help at church. I've been there for thirteen years or more now. My jobs have been different over the years. For a while I was the director of the toys for needy kids program. Every year I did fundraising and gathered $3,000 to $5,000. I put a lot of my own money in. I never forgot about that friend who took Mom, Joni, Donnie, and me to Christmas dinner that night. With my fundraising, the church bought brand new toys and food baskets. We welcomed families from all the way up to White River Junction in Vermont. We gave each child three brand new toys, gift wrapped.

When I'm up to it, I play the conga at church and clean up the restrooms, mop the floor, and vacuum the church for Sunday services. I delivered food for twelve straight years, but recently had to resign from that, too. I just don't have the energy to stand for long periods. You have to meet certain requirements, and I can't meet them. I might not even see next Christmas.

Pastor Bruce has always trusted me. I told him straight up when we met that I am a convict. They had to run my background because of the toys for needy kids work. I have several policemen who are friends. Ted is a retired Massachusetts State Trooper. Sam is the former Chief of Police in Grafton. We laugh about it and say, "Thirty years ago we'd be shooting at each other."

I always say, "It wouldn't have been personal." I probably would have been laughing my butt off while I shot at them thirty years ago. I wouldn't laugh now. I wouldn't shoot now.

BROTHER-IN-LAW

TEN YEARS AFTER I MOVED BACK EAST, PAUL DIED. Paul had Lewy Body dementia. He wasn't just a brother-in-law to me; he was a brother. We loved each other in that way. He confided in me. He talked to me about things he wouldn't talk to the kids about. I brought him to the hospital that last time. His stomach was swollen up again, and he said, "Bob, I need to go to hospital."

I said, "Do you want an ambulance?"

He said, "No. I want you to take me."

We left for the hospital around four in the afternoon, and he kept asking me all the way there, "Do you want to stop?" I was smoking then, and he kept asking, "Do you want to stop and have a cigarette first?"

I said, "No. You're more important than a cigarette, Paul. I'm going to get you there."

Three times he asked me if I wanted to stop, and I said, "No." He really didn't want to go in. I think he knew in his heart that this was the last time. In his hospital room, I was reading him the Bible and we were praying together at about one in the morning. I thought he fell asleep, but he had actually slipped into a coma. He died the next day. I was heartbroken. I felt like I did when my kid brother died. Bruce conducted Paul's dedication of life service. There were more people than I'd ever seen in that church. It was packed. The family sold the house, so I had to move my camper to some friends' house, then to the church.

CANOE

BEING A CHRISTAN DOESN'T PREVENT YOU FROM HAVING HARD STUFF LIKE GRIEF, ACCIDENTS, AND ILLNESSES, BUT YOU CAN SEE MIRACLES IF YOU PAY ATTENTION. I've seen so many. I've experienced so many. My driver's license and my eyesight are just two of the miracles that have happened to me since I've been back east. When I was attending the Grafton church, every summer Pastor Tom and his family camped up at Littleton on Moore Reservoir. They kept a trailer parked there year round and spent a month there every year. I usually went up the last week or two and camped near them. They always reserved a spot for me between a bunch of boulders. It had a big, almost a nest, of pine needles where I'd put my tent.

One weekend I planned to head out Friday night to get up there, but one thing after another happened. Every time I turned around something else came up, and I couldn't leave. I finally called them and said, "I won't be up until Monday or Tuesday of next week. There's just one thing after another. I don't understand why I'm so busy."

Sunday I went to church and one of the elders in the church came up to me and said, "You were supposed to be up there with Tom and Nancy this weekend, weren't you?"

I said, "Yes."

He said, "Well, it's a good thing you didn't go up there because a microburst hit, and it took a down a huge ponderosa pine near their campsite." The elder said, "It's a miracle you weren't there."

I said, "Well, everything that could go wrong went wrong. I had no choice not to stay here until Monday."

I found out from Tom that the tree fell right into the pine needles where my tent would have been. In the middle of the night it would have crushed me to death. He measured the trunk of that tree as five feet thick. That was scary.

Another miracle took place in the same area. I was up in Moore Reservoir with two friends. I was out in the middle of the lake in a canoe just paddling away up the channel. I remember thinking, *My faith is so strong, God, that right now I believe I could walk on water.* That is one thing I will never say again because it was like an invincible hand came down, grabbed that canoe, flipped it up on its side, and dumped me out into the water. I was fully dressed, with shoes on. One pocket was full of change and the other was full of nuts and bolts. I always carry nuts and bolts with me in case something breaks down.

I sank so far down the water was black. I remember thinking, *Well, all I've got to do is take one breath and I'm out of here.* Then a voice screamed down inside of me and said, "No!" The next thing I knew I was on the surface. The water was cold. I got cold water cramps in my side and in my left arm. I grabbed onto the canoe. It had sunk a little, and was full of water, but it had flotation devices attached to it so it stayed up somewhat. I grabbed a huge coffee cup out of the hull and tried to bail water with one hand while I held on to the canoe side with the other.

I wound up kicking off my clothes and throwing them into the lake. I started swimming on my back, and the cold water cramps went away. I swam a little, then pulled the canoe toward me, then swam a little more. For 45 minutes I swam like that until I was about two miles from shore. I was exhausted by that point. I said, "God, if You need to take me home now, if I'm meant to drown, let's not mess around. Let's just do it, but if I'm not meant to die at this point, I need Your help because I am totally exhausted right now." I was drifting farther and farther toward the main channel. It's a big lake. It's a big, big lake. From where we camped it was almost five miles to the dam and open water. I started singing "Amazing Grace" at the top of my voice. There I was, totally naked, pulling a canoe, and singing a hymn. After ten minutes or so, I thought, *Well, let's see if I'm making any headway.* I will never forget this. I turned around and looked, and I was 100 yards from shore. I have no idea how I traveled almost two miles in ten minutes.

Soon, my foot brushed a rock, and I was able to stand up. I had never felt that good. The water was up to my neck, but I was able to stand up on that rock and take a long breath. I emptied the canoe of all of the water. All I lost were my shoes, my clothes, and my fishing rod. My tackle box floated. I pushed the canoe and swam behind it, kicking my feet. Then I got in the canoe and paddled to the shore.

My friends were just getting ready to call the sheriff's department. They said they looked out there and could see me, and then they didn't see me anymore. After about an hour they got concerned. One asked, "Bob, where have you been?" I told them what happened. My friend said, "Man, that's a miracle because we saw you out there in a canoe one minute, and the next minute you were gone. That was over an hour ago."

I said, "Yes. It was a miracle." I told what had happened. I must have looked like a highspeed motorboat pulling that canoe across the water because it went two miles in ten minutes. I guess nobody else saw that. The boat flipped because of what I said about walking on water. Now I know better.

PATTY

NOW I'M HONEST WITH GOD AND MYSELF AND OTHER PEOPLE. My relationship with Jesus is my number one priority. There's a nice lady named Patty who lives in a trailer park right up behind the church. She's two years older than I am, and a tiny woman at five feet four inches and 90 pounds. She's a cowgirl. She likes to go to the rodeo, and she survived a bad, bad marriage. She lost her children, too. Her husband alienated them from her. She knows heartache.

We met when she walked through the field between the trailer park and the church. My buddy and I were out there, and she came up and started talking to us. The church had an acre of land that was landlocked on one side by the trailer park. The owners of the park (the residents) wanted to buy the acre from the church for $25,000. We had a meeting about it. Bruce and I were in total agreement just to give it to them. So, we gave the trailer park residents the land. They loved that. When Bruce retired, they all chipped in and gave him a gift of $3,000 for the church. It was written up in the newspaper and we got an anonymous donation of $5,000 from someone who liked what we did.

Patty wanted me to move in with her, and I did for a week, but then it got kind of weird. She asked me one time about my baby brother, and I don't like to go into detail about little Paul or when he died. It's still painful. To this day, I don't watch movies that show a child dying. It brings me down. I explained to her how I've lost people and been hurt in marriage. I told her I don't let myself love people anymore.

She said, "Well, you've made me love you."

I said, "Wait a minute. Time out. I told you right from the start and from the first time I met you that I'm not looking for romance. I'm incapable of that kind of love anymore. I will be your friend. I'll be the best friend you've ever had in your life, but I won't allow myself to love that way again." I got all my stuff out of her house, picked up Black Cat, and went back to my camper.

Women like me. I don't know why. When I look at myself in the mirror I think, *If I were a woman and I asked me out, by the time I got* done laughing, I'd say, *"Absolutely not, under no circumstances."* All my life I've had a low opinion of myself. I think I'm butt ugly. That's why I never asked anybody out. I didn't want to be rejected. My problem was that when I was with in love with a woman, like my girlfriend in California and like with Lil, I loved and didn't hold back. I put the woman in my life on a pedestal and would do anything for her. Even with Louise and Rhonda, I trusted completely, and I got burned. My last marriage killed any feelings of love I've ever had, and I haven't allowed myself to feel that kind of love again.

Patty was very angry and upset. She called and asked me if she could come over. She asked if she could at least feed Black Cat in the mornings. I said, "Yes, I don't have a problem with you coming over, Patty. I'm not angry at you at all. I understand where you're coming from. I don't want to hurt you. You are a good person. One of the reasons I don't want to get close is that I am dying. I don't want someone falling in love with me now only to watch me die and have to grieve. That's a horrible way to be hurt. But, I will be your best friend."

She asked, "Will you give me a hug?"

I said, "I will always have a hug for you."

DYING

RIGHT NOW, IT'S TOTALLY OVERCAST. It just stopped snowing, but it's going to start back up again. The temperature is dropping, and it's getting cold. We've got about six inches so far, and we're supposed to get more. It was freezing last night, and this morning a really wet snow came down with big flakes that didn't take long to build. The weatherman says New Hampshire might get up to a foot right here. As overcast as it is, there's no way the snow is finished. It's going to start up again. Another storm is coming on the weekend. We'll see what happens. It's one of those good nights to be inside and not have to go anywhere.

I'm in a rehabilitation facility, kind of like a nursing home, right now. The doctors want to keep me as close to the dialysis center as possible. Joni has come up from Massachusetts for a couple of my operations. Bruce checks on me all the time, but he's not in town anymore. I wish I had Black Cat with me. I got to see him at church one day. He is mad at me. He wouldn't sit in my lap, but I held him for a while. He's confused. He probably thinks I deserted him. Patty is keeping him for me.

Doctors are telling me now that I'm retaining a lot of water. I've gained over four kilos of weight, and I guess it's putting a lot of stress on my heart. I could have a heart attack. So, I have cut down my fluid intake. I just chew ice. I usually have a bowl of cold cereal in the morning. I used to drink a glass of milk at lunch and dinner, plus a cup of tea, but I have to give up one or the other. Maybe I'll have milk at lunch and tea at dinner. One day, the nurses forgot to give me a snack before I took insulin. When I told the dialysis technician, she said, "That's very dangerous. You could go into insulin shock really quickly."

Being dependent on others is hard. I order my lunch every day, but I almost never get what I order. I usually just ask for a salad and a glass of milk or tea. If they bring tea, they bring hot water but no tea bag. They always forget salt and pepper. Simple stuff. The medical staff here is good to me, though, and at Dartmouth-Hitchcock, I'm treated like I'm the governor. The Dartmouth nurses and doctors and palliative care unit are awesome. I can't say enough about my primary care physician Dr. Glowa and her husband Don Colash. One doctor comes on breaks and sits in my room and talks with me. I always fill out the little report cards and send them in with good reviews. The hospital gave me financial assistance because all I have now is Social Security and Medicare. I'm not on the kidney transplant list because of my financial and insurance situation. Dr. Glowa got really upset about that, but I told her, "It's okay. I have a friend who got a kidney from his sister decades ago and he starts off every morning with a pile of pills to swallow." I have a whole bag full of pills that I have to take already, some of them three times a day, some just after dialysis, some twice a day, and then insulin. I get tired. I usually have to eat something first, and then I forget to take them.

I know I don't have that much longer to go. I can feel it. I'm weaker right now than I've ever been in my life. I've been incredibly blessed with a lot of strength until the last year. Now, to walk down to the elevators, I have to stop a couple of times because it hurts my legs. That's because there's no circulation going down to them. My back is constantly in pain, and headaches are driving me crazy. They are caused by damage to the base of my brain. If I don't catch one before it gets to my ears (because it works its way forward) and take medicine, once it gets to my eyes, that's it. I just have to grit my teeth and bear it. There's nothing that touches the pain. A tumor affects my right eye, so when I read I have to keep my right eye closed. It's the only way I can read. I've been going without sleep for about four years now. I lie down at about eight o'clock so tired I can't keep my eyes open, but by midnight I'm wide awake. I fall back asleep around two and wake up 30 minutes later. I learned not to sleep past three since I have to get up at five to go to dialysis. I just stay awake and get a cup of coffee.

I'm 72 now. The kidney doctor talked to me about the reality of the situation. He said, "It is your decision whether or not you continue dialysis. If you stop, we expect that the end will be very quick. Your kidneys are completely done now, so we'll make you comfortable.

That's it. We won't revive you. We won't give you any treatments. You'll last from about two weeks to a month, but no more than a month."

I will slip into a coma and then never wake up. He said that's a good way to go, a peaceful way to go. Sometimes, I have no desire to live anymore. I feel like I'm in a hole, the walls are smooth so there's no climbing out, and I can't get a foothold. I look up to the top of the hole to earth, and I don't see a light. I see darkness and more darkness. One thing after another is starting to happen now. My body is going, but I'm really pushing myself to get it back up. It's hard on the days that I have dialysis. I can't do therapy on those days because I'm so worn out. In therapy, I walk with a nurse who follows me. She holds onto a belt that's wrapped around me. I hate being sick and being considered an invalid. I have to get my strength back so I can take care of myself again, be with Black Cat, and because Jesus has one more job for me here.

A biker brother recently came to see me. When he was about to leave he said, "I probably won't see you again."

I said, "Yes, you will. I'm not checking out that quick."

It's been a while since I've ridden a motorcycle. I guess around 1996 was the last time. My favorite thing to do was ride wide open, feeling the wind on my face and in my hair, going as fast as I could go. I would love to ride again.

BROTHER

UNTIL MY BABY BROTHER PAUL DIED, EVEN UP TO THE FUNERAL, I DIDN'T COMPREHEND DEATH. The only death I was familiar with as a child came from TV. I watched an actor get killed in a series, but the next week he would be on another show. I was so young. I just thought, *Paul didn't really die. He faked it. I'll see him tomorrow.* At his funeral, I walked up front and looked in the casket, and the first thing that I noticed was his lips were sewn together. I bent down and kissed him on the cheek. His skin was ice cold. Then I lost it. I totally lost it. I don't remember much except two men carrying me out. I don't remember going to the cemetery. I don't remember going to the wake.

Paul was diagnosed in 1954 and was in and out of the hospital until he died in 1959. He was held back in first grade for missing so much school, and then the district just excused him. They realized how sick he was and how heavy the situation was for our family.

At one point his birthday was coming up. We were dirt poor, and he was really sick. I wanted to buy him something. I was talking to my teacher about it, and he said, "Well, why don't you take up a collection?" So I did. I started going around showing people a little paper that I'd written about Paul. I knocked on people's doors and said, "Would you like to help a little boy who is dying in a hospital?"

The next thing I knew, my whole class was collecting, and then Joni and Donnie started collecting. We raised well over $1,000. We bought all kinds of toys and things for Paul and had to use two or three taxi cabs to bring everything to the hospital. Then we had to get help unloading and taking it all up to his room. Paul picked out all the toys he wanted, then Mom let Donnie, Joni, and me each keep one toy. We gave the rest to the children's ward at the hospital.

My brother had two last requests that were very publicized. His first goal was to make it to his confirmation. I don't know how, but this got to the television and newspapers. They both did special pieces on Paul. Maybe Mom reached out to people. Everyone tried to help Paul. A priest, I think his name was Bishop Sheen, came from New York City and gave Paul his holy confirmation.

The other request was that he wanted to be a Boy Scout and make it to Eagle Scout. I don't know how they found out about it. Maybe Mom contacted someone. The Boy Scouts of America donated him a full Cub Scout uniform with the ribbon to every merit badge. They made him an honorary Cub and gave him a beautiful ring. He was buried in his Cub Scout uniform.

My baby brother Paul died 60 years ago, and it still hurts to talk about it. I look at that last picture taken of us, and I now know that I will see my brother again, thanks to my Lord.

I never forgot what my mom told me when she got home from saying goodbye to Paul. I asked her, "Did he say anything before he died?"

She said, "Yes, he said the most amazing thing."

"What did he say?" I asked.

She said, "He was staring out the window. Then he looked over at me and said, 'Does Jesus love me?' I said, 'Yes, of course He loves you. Why?' Paul took a deep breath, looked out the window again, and said, 'Because He's coming for me right now.' Then Paul let his breath out, and he was gone."

At the end of that vision I had a few years back, the Lord said, "Once you complete the third task, you'll have to make a decision." I don't know what that decision will be. I don't know. I will know when it happens. I haven't met the third person yet. When I do, my assignment will be over. Then I'll have a choice to make, and I'll do whatever my Lord commands me to do. I will know when it's my turn to go. I will look up, and Jesus will hold out his hand to me and say, "Come on, child. It's time for you to come home."

Made in the USA
Monee, IL
01 February 2020